A SENSE OF THE
COUNTRY

LINDA BURGESS

A SENSE OF THE
COUNTRY

A SEASONAL GUIDE TO DECORATING YOUR HOME
WITH FLOWERS, FRUITS AND NATURAL OBJECTS

WITH A TEXT BY SUSAN CONDER

LITTLE, BROWN AND COMPANY
BOSTON TORONTO LONDON

FOR MY FAMILY

FIRST U.S. EDITION

First published in Great Britain in 1990
by The Octopus Publishing Group/Amazon Publishing Ltd.

Library of Congress Catalog Number 89-63096

10 9 8 7 6 5 4 3 2 1

Produced by Mandarin Offset
Printed and bound in Hong Kong

CONTENTS

INTRODUCTION

Flowers have been so good to me, and photographing them is one way to communicate the mystery and goodness of life, to hold on to them forever, rather like possessing a piece of time. For when I put flowers and objects together, I notice that the still life becomes something like a living painting, suggesting to me that flowers have their own language, that they speak of life itself: colourful, exquisite, perfect and imperfect, disappointing, changing and fading. Flowers show such resilence and power, while also being fragile — even ugly at times.

Quiet survivors in a world where they are not always welcome, flowers are often used merely as the right things to be seen at the right time and not as fully integrated friends. We are not considerate of nature, but more often arrogantly ask it to 'please move over' and make more room for us. The offering in a restaurant of a tired carnation or dusty silk fuchsias reminds me of how much we would miss their steady presence if they were not there. And gone are the days when we could go for a walk and pick wild flowers from the country: sad but true. We must now be the nurturers.

What warm familiarity there is standing under a favourite cherry tree, falling under its spell, or to see a corner of a neighbour's garden in yet another year, surrendering its colour and gifts; fragile snowdrops with their persistence pushing up through the cold February ground; or the obstinate, firm, early irises, their leaves so daring and strong as to almost pierce the hand. Through flowers we are able to take part in the changing seasons and it is only natural therefore that we should include them into our lives: not to do so would run the risk of our becoming ever remoter from ourselves. Flowers can help our home and senses to be more fused and part of the country and the country more a part of us. We can appreciate the suspense of very early spring, the explosive life of summer, the quiet resignation of autumn, and the withdrawal and renewal of winter. Flowers in a room can convey inspiration and comfort, a focal point for the senses. One bloom in a jam jar can bring the joy of the country right here into our homes, blocking out for a while a busy, stressful, polluted world.

I hope this book will encourage you anew to love flowers, to linger with them, to enjoy the fineness of their deliberate design, their associations with your favourite objects, the touch of their petals, the coolness of their leaves.

The key to everything is simplicity, go for what you genuinely enjoy. I adore colour, it mesmerises me and shocks me. I love the honest, flat orange of calendulas, the bruised purple of figs, putting together objects that harmonise. Find out which shape sings its own song, by being solitary or closer to the company of another object. I find inspiration from every direction I look, whether it is moss-covered paving in an ancient garden or rain-covered bunches of florists' roses wrapped in their celophane. Almost everything pleads to be noticed.

So let us surrender to flowers, let them permeate our thoughts, saturate our senses and warm our hearts.

Linda Burgess

ree-range Plymouth Rocks and
Rhode Island Reds momentarily
ignore an unexpected item in their run.
They are naturally inquisitive creatures, and the
freshly picked tulips, left *in situ*, would soon be
pecked, pulled from the tub and scattered.

SPRING

I have seen foreign flowers in hothouses of the most beautiful nature, but I do not care a straw for them. The simple flowers of our spring are what I want to see again.

JOHN KEATS, 1795–1821

A sinkful of spring potential
contains single scarlet and crimson and
double yellow tulips and narcissi. A
basket of several potted florists' cyclamens awaits
display, and freesias hang upside down to air dry.
Tulips and narcissi, like most bulbous flowers,
should have their stems re-cut and be given a long
drink of water before being placed on display.
Frequent re-cutting of the stems extends their life.

There are so many clichés about the renewal of growth and rebirth in spring that, as a season, it almost smacks of a massive public relations exercise. The springtime of one's life is said to be full of potential. 'Spring' also describes a natural source of water and an energetic upward leap, indirectly adding purity and vitality to the seasonal meaning. Spring is biologically rousing, with increased temperatures and light levels causing increased activity, especially reproduction, in many plants and animals.

For most people, spring does mark an annual renewal of hope, whether on the romantic or professional front, or simply starting a new diet, buying new clothes or changing hair styles. Traditional spring cleaning often dispenses with winter's passivity along with accumulated winter dust.

Officially, 21 March is the vernal equinox and the first day of spring. To the romantic, St Valentine's Day, once thought to be the day when birds mate for the season, marks the advent of spring (The Roman fertility festival of Lupercalia was held on the 15th.)

*I*n design terms, a group of three is usually more interesting than a pair or foursome. Here, clear-pink double tulips and lenten roses (*Helleborus orientalis*) are joined by branches of spring-flowering *Chaenomeles*, also known as japonica, or flowering quince. Like the spring palette itself, *Chaenomeles* and tulips range in colour from white, uncomplicated pastels and intense primary colours to subtle shades and tints.

A close up of the double tulips and more richly hued lenten roses (*Helleborus orientalis*) on a sun-filled spring windowsill. Lenten roses are notoriously difficult to condition; here, the problem is solved by displaying the flower heads alone in a shallow, water-filled dish. Like hydrangeas, hellebore flowers change colour as they age, and, like hydrangeas, all stages of their development are attractive.

Wholesale florists double the price of red hybrid tea roses just before St Valentine's Day, knowing that the compulsion to give one's beloved a red rose on 14 February is stronger for many people than their sense of consumer fair play.

Easter, commemorating Christ's resurrection, is a movable feast, also with connotations of the start of spring. Like Christmas, the timing of Easter was probably an exercise in subtle religious subterfuge, fixed initially to absorb some of the fervour of earlier pagan spring rituals, as well as the Jewish festival of Passover.

The transition from winter to summer weather can occur as smoothly as an even gradient on a graph, but is usually a series of unpredictable highs and lows, when a cold spell can undo the previous benefits of days or weeks of mild weather. March winds often devastate plants that survived the cold of January and February, and April droughts can be as fatal as those of high summer.

Spring is traditionally the busiest time of year in the garden, with lifting, dividing, planting and re-planting, sowing and staking and tying up to do. There is a special sense of urgency, as certain tasks require particular weather conditions or plants in a particular stage of development, and it is easy to miss the right moment. To meet the increased demands of gardeners, some garden centres have late-night shopping, in the manner of the pre-Christmas frenzy.

For cut-flower displays, spring presents many more options than winter, whether the source of material is a garden or a florist's shop. The increase in natural heat and light which encourages plants to grow reduces the cost of commercial flower production, and therefore the price of florists' flowers.

SPRING COLOURS

Spring marks the slow, then increasingly quicker, transition in the garden from predominantly greys and browns to basically green. Those with weekend cottages will begin to notice a marked difference in their gardens from one weekend to the next, reminiscent of 24-hour time-lapse photography which records the growth and unfolding of flowers. Deciduous woods change dramatically from a grey-brown haze to pale green, and by April lawns are fresh green and dormant herbaceous perennials, having pushed vertically upwards, unfold their leaves to hide the bare earth.

Interior designers use the term 'colourways' to describe the various colour combinations available in a particular pattern of fabric, carpet or wallpaper. There are three main 'colourways' of spring: the soft pastels of early spring bulbs and biennials such as chionodoxa, forget-me-not and Canterbury bells; the bright, clear primary colours of many bedding plants and spring-flowering shrubs, such as polyanthus, forsythia, doronicum and flowering quince; and the rich, subtle tones of flowers such as auricula, fritillary, Lenten rose (*Helleborus orientalis*) and many wallflowers. Unlike fabric colourways, each neatly self-contained, most gardens have a mixture of all of them. Florists tend to favour pastels and pure, primary colours, leaving the subtle colours for gardens to provide.

Tulips are used here as part of a study
in primary colours and black and white.
The Kelim carpet and patchwork cushions
create richly varied geometric patterns, in contrast to
the natural forms of the flowers. Tulip
stems continue to grow after being cut, often in
graceful curves, and the flowers move towards the
light, so a display of tulips is constantly changing.
This can be awkward with formal arrangements, but
delightful with informal ones, as here.

This montage of fresh polyanthus, pansy and hyacinth florets on a background of artists' colours is short-lived and self-indulgent, but it is pleasant to experiment with small units of colour without having to think about an end-product. Children often behead garden flowers to make private patterns of colour on the ground, to the dismay of their parents but obviously fulfilling some basic need. Here, the interplay of natural flower forms and dabs of paint can be further enlivened by shadows.

White, yellow and blue continue from late winter, since many winter flowers ignore the vernal equinox and carry on as before – snowdrops, winter aconites and netted iris among them. Spring snowflakes (*Leucojum* species) and double daisies follow; later come the greenish white stars of Bethlehem (*Ornithogalum nutans*, *O. umbellatum*). So-called clock plants, stars of Bethlehem shut early each day and in dull weather. In America they are known as 'nap at noon', or 'ten o'clock lady', and considered invasive weeds. Stars of Bethlehem are long-lasting when cut and, densely massed, make a good ruffle round a centre of brightly coloured flowers.

Green is taken for granted in spring foliage and lawns, but green flowers have an oddity value and intrigue similar to that of black flowers. Green hellebores – *Helleborus foetidus*, *H. lividus corsicus*, *H. viridis* – overlap with the winter species, and continue well into spring. Norway maple's clusters of green flowers appear before its leaves; the black branches in flower are attractive on their own or with tulips or daffodils. The spikes of tiny green bells of fringecup,

Artistic licence in pursuit of beautiful images: cut snowdrops and decanted polyanthus capture the spirit, if not the horticultural reality, of spring. Conventionally planted, the snowdrops are set against their leaves, and polyanthus foliage is angled to maximize each leaf's exposure to sunlight.

Tellima grandiflora, can add linear grace to more massive flowers. In late spring there are *Viridiflora* tulips, green auriculas, green arums, lady's mantle, *Euphorbia robbiae* and immature hydrangea and guelder rose flowers (*Viburnum opulus*).

Yellow is particularly associated with spring: sunny, fresh, luminous, lively, young and friendly. Pale yellow is a socially acceptable alternative to pale pink and pale blue for baby clothes, handy if presents have to be bought before an infant's sex is known; gentlemen are said to prefer blondes, epitomized by Marilyn Monroe who, with her yellow hair, embodied the powerful combination of innocence and sexuality; and the yellow brick road held excitement for Dorothy and her friends in *The Wizard of Oz*. Yellow has its share of negative connotations, too: cowardice, deceit, danger and treachery, with the 'yellow press' symbolizing the worst aspects of journalism. The Victorians made a heavy-handed attempt to burden yellow flowers with negative connotations in the *Language of Flowers*, a romantic, secret system of communication through

affodils, that come before the swallow dares, and take The winds of March with beauty . . .'
So wrote Shakespeare in *A Winter's Tale*. Yellow is probably the colour most often associated with spring, and narcissi, in all its forms, the most archetypally spring flower. In traditional flower-arranging wisdom, narcissi don't work well in mixed displays. Here, they are set out, cultivar by cultivar, in a pretty floral line-up.

flowers. Yellow daffodils, for example, were said to stand for egotism, yellow roses for jealousy and decreased love, and evening primroses for inconstancy. The language never really worked, as the many 'dictionaries' published in England and America to meet popular demand gave wildly varied meanings for each flower. Yellow flowers, in any case, have long since shed this artificial

notoriety, and the gift of yellow flowers is as welcome as those of any other hue. Interestingly, though, yellow clothes are hard to wear, for most people.

Unlike the heavy, old-gold yellows of autumn, spring's yellows tend to be light, often with the tiniest tinge of green, and occasionally appear cool. The exceptions include yellow-orange wallflowers,

*Y*ellow and purple crocuses fill a spring
window box. Complementary colours,
yellow and purple in combination are
attractive to pollinating insects, if somewhat tricky
in interior design and fashion!

crocuses and polyanthus, which sometimes look out of place against softer, clearer spring colours. Like white, yellows in a garden are visible from a distance, especially against a dark or dull green background, or in a shady corner. Though shade indoors is usually less pronounced than outdoor shadows, yellow flowers can light up darkish corners or niches.

The colour violet is equally associated with spring, in violets and pansies, early-flowering species clematis, pasque flowers, lilacs and aubrieta, purple crocuses and bedding plants. In its pure hue, violet is a heavy colour, visually recessive and not able to add long-distance sparkle to a garden. It is more easily appreciated at close range, which makes it most suitable for cut-flower displays. Violet's over-tones, like those of black, are sombre, heavy, and melancholy, and mature rather than youthful. There is a sense of mystery attached to purple, perhaps an inkling of evil. An archetypally high-Victorian colour, violet became established as the colour of deep mourning.

Pansies (*Viola × wittrockiana*) are perfectly matched with a hand-painted Clarice Cliff Art Deco tea cup. Florists', or garden, pansies were bred in the early nineteenth century, reputedly by the gardeners of Lady Mary Bennett, who crossed annual heartease (*Viola tricolor*) with perennial mountain violet (*V. lutea*) and a large Dutch variety. By the mid-nineteenth century there were over 400 named pansies. Charles Darwin noted with interest the pansies' transformation over twenty years from small, irregular blossoms to huge, velvety, blooms.

*W*inter-
flowering *Iris
reticulata* continue
into spring; here, they
make an elegant multi-
tiered display, given
formal impact by its
setting. Small scale
winter- and spring-
flowering bulbs can be
displayed loosely, so that
the individual form of
each flower shows, as in
the cluster of
accompanying grape
hyacinths, or as a dense
texture, spreading as far
as supplies allow.

*S*nowdrops, narcissi, skimmia
flowers and marbled cyclamen leaves
offer seasonal condiments for the eyes!
Violets, scillas, spring anemones, chionodoxas, lily
of the valley, heartsease, epimedium foliage, sprigs of
almond, plum, crab-apple or cherry blossom . . . the
possible combinations in a miniature multiple
container are infinite.

Violet clothes followed black in the lengthy process of grieving at
which the Victorians excelled, led by Queen Victoria after the death
of her beloved Albert.

Violet softened with white becomes mauve, lavender and lilac,
subtle or crude according to the proportions of red, blue and white.
The higher the proportion of white, the more these colours attract
the eye. Some pale-purple tones border on the grey – Lenten rose
(*Helleborus orientalis*) and pasque flower, for example – especially
under incandescent light.

Yellow and violet are complementary colours on the colour
wheel and form a combination particularly associated with spring,
especially Easter. When the colours occur within a single flower,
such as pansy and heartsease, or Johnny-jump-up, the purpose is to
attract pollinating insects. Both in the garden and in the wild, the
combination can occur in large-scale juxtapositions of different
species or varieties of the same plant, as well as of totally different

A golden mixture of tulips, daffodils
and fragrant narcissi, informally
displayed in a low wickerwork basket,
capture and intensify the pale, early
spring light. The infinitely well-behaved pig
contemplating the flowers has other food for
thought: the last of the stored winter apples ripening
on the windowsill.

plants: purple aubrieta and yellow alyssum in a rockery or dry-stone wall; laburnum and lilac flowering in unison; purple heather and yellow gorse; drifts of yellow and purple crocus in a lawn.

Because certain flowers bloom at the same time, it is tempting to think that they must look 'right' together, and be inherently pleasing to the eye. While there is often colour harmony among plants flowering at the same time in their native environment, harsh juxtapositions are entirely possible in a garden.

Most gardens contain as many exotics as native plants. Exotics, confused by the weather, may flower earlier or later than they would in their native habitat, and in any case their colour is often meant to attract pollinators different from those in their adoptive home. The line between native and exotic is also blurred. *Rhododendron ponticum*, for example, one of the main sources of purple flowers in spring, grows wild, even invasively, over many parts of England, but is actually a mid-eighteenth-century garden escape, originally from

Asia Minor, having found English conditions ideal for naturalizing. To the purist, rhododendrons' huge flowers are 'un-English', and will remain so, however long its provenance.

Many garden cultivars do not occur in nature at all; the huge colour range of hybrid hyacinths, tulips and wallflowers, for example, is full of potential, but not always successful in combination, even within a single seed packet or box of bedding plants.

Some people do gasp with pleasure at the sight of purple and yellow *en masse* in a spring garden, while others dislike it. Few interior decoration schemes and clothing fashions are based on yellow and purple, always a good indication of what people feel comfortable with. Certainly, *haute couturiers*, occasionally show purple and yellow ensembles, but these seem more for shock and publicity value than anything else, since while they may appear on the covers of colour magazines, and fashion writers lavish praise, the outfits rarely appear off the catwalk.

Proportion also affects how complementary colours are perceived. The tiny yellow-orange stamens in the centre of a purple crocus are thrilling, but that same purple combined with an equal amount of that same yellow-orange in, say, a mixed-colour crocus bed, might seem crude. The tiny orange eye and violet feathering of the white *Viola septentrionalis* is another example of how small amounts of complementary colours can please the eye, set against a larger, neutral background.

SPRING FLOWERS

Early spring-flowering bulbs such as scilla, crocus and chionodoxa retain the small scale of winter flowers, keeping themselves close to the ground for protection against the weather. Both the Algerian iris (*I. unguicularis*) and many early crocus produce stemless flowers and dull-coloured outer buds, perhaps as protection from hungry sparrows. Alpine plants such as *Androsace* and *Saxifraga* species are also short-stemmed, as a defence against their harsh native environment. Many early-spring flowers, including cowslip primroses, primroses, bluebells and violets, inhabit woodlands or the shelter of dormant hedgerows.

Cut-flower displays based on these garden and wild herbaceous flowers in early spring are therefore inherently limited in height, although, like fabric, they can extend widthways in a display – from an egg cup filled with a dozen violets to a large, enamelled dish filled with many times that number. Such early-spring displays encourage the observation of floral detail: the markings on a petal, the arrangement of stamens, the colour change as a blossom ages.

Daffodils have a winter presence in florists' shops, but a natural affinity to spring. Expert flower-arrangers generally advise against mixing daffodils with other flowers in cut displays, perhaps because daffodil blooms are so adamantly front-facing and right-angled in relation to the stems, which are themselves poker-straight. The flowers tend to look better with just foliage or branches: hazel or birch in catkin; the near-black, narrow leaves of mondo grass,

*N*arcissi in variety – trumpet,
large- and small-cupped, double and
poet's – cram a double-handled jug. Those
of complex parentage tend to lose in simple charm
what they gain in size, unusual shape or colour; the
modest single wild daffodil, or Lent lily, *Narcissus
pseudonarcissus*, is, to many people, the ideal. A
raised bowl of lemons continues the yellow theme.
Yellow powdered chalk is rubbed on to the vase, as if
the narcissi themselves cast a yellow glow.

rape hyacinths are combined with red-and-white feathered parrot tulips showing 'broken' colour patterns. Tulip patterning is caused by a virus (unlike the genetic variation which causes 'breaks' in *Dianthus*). Patterning has always been an obsession among tulip breeders, with 'rose', 'bizarre', 'bizard' and 'byblomen' indicating different combinations of ground colours and markings. Seedling tulips produce plain flowers for up to eight years before 'breaking' into pattern, which explains the high prices of 'breeder' bulbs. The 'breaks' are unpredictable, so there is an element of risk and chance, which helps explain seventeenth-century 'Tulipmania' and the renewed interest in the plant during the nineteenth century.

The stems of these pink tulips have
been allowed to curve at will. Tulips,
especially large-flowered hybrids, can be
enormously voluptuous, like vessels waiting to be
filled. The Victorians recognized this and also knew
of the eighteenth-century Turkish tulip feasts, where
Sultans chose their favourites from among the harem
displayed in a tulip-filled courtyard. In their attempt
to draw moral lessons from nature, the Victorians,
for example in the book *Flora's Gems* (1837),
accused the tulip of being garish, haughty, scentless
and disdainful, and in the end, black at heart.

Ophiopogon planiscapus 'Nigrescens'; or variegated bamboo foliage, for example. Their own leaves also suit them, but, unfortunately, florists' daffodils are most often sold without foliage. In season, daffodils are so inexpensive that massing dozens in a large container is not an extravagance, although they are short-lived, particularly in hot rooms.

The archetypal mid-spring flowers are tulips, hyacinths, polyanthus, pansies and auriculas. The huge number of cultivars available is largely a result of the devoted flower breeding done by nineteenth-century English working-class florists. (Summer's pinks, carnations and dahlias owe their diversity to the same source.) 'Floristry' originally referred, not to the commercial sale of cut flowers, but to the amateur cultivation of individual flowers, to improve the breed and achieve perfection, defined in terms of symmetry, size and markings. The hobby came to England with migrant Flemish weavers escaping religious persecution. Because many plants could be grown in a small space, the hobby suited the tiny gardens and allotments that were available. As *The Gardener and Practical Florist* of 1843 noted:

> *The culture of the tulip, polyanthus, auricula,*
> *carnation, pink, ranunculus & c., was even a*
> *few years ago confined chiefly to the most*
> *illiterate class of society, and to their skill and*
> *perseverance we are mainly indebted for some*
> *of the most beautiful varieties now grown; yet*
> *these persons knew no more about botany or*
> *general floriculture than the man in the moon.*

To be suitable for 'floristry' work, flowers had to grow easily from seed, produce varied seedlings and be capable of vegetative propagation once a desired strain had been created. The 'floristry' craze reached its peak in the mid-nineteenth century. Many of the cultivars have since disappeared, but enough remain to commemorate the skill and devotion of their breeders.

Cut tulips are available commercially from autumn onwards, but early forced types often have a severely limited colour range and an anaemic quality: more tokens of tulips than anything else. As their true season approaches choice increases, double-flowered tulips appear, and the blooms are more generous and convincing. Garden tulips offer the greatest choice, and the early species tulips – *Tulipa aucherana*, *T. biflora*, *T. clusiana*, *T. tarda* – have a modest grace missing from many of the larger cultivars. At flower shows held on the last day of spring (whether they are of local horticultural societies or national exhibitions), unusual and beautiful cut flowers are often sold off cheaply or given away. Tulips and other flowers from this source may only have a couple of days' display life left, but many other pleasures are even shorter-lived.

Just as daffodils' poker-straight stems affect their use in cut-flower displays, so the naturally elongating, curving stems of tulips

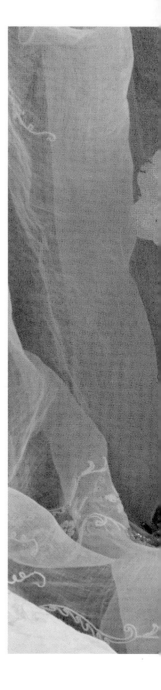

demand thought. It was once conventional floristry (in the twentieth-century sense of the word) practice to wire tulip stems to control their shape. Less drastic is to wrap the flowers, heads and all, tightly in newspaper, and soak them overnight in deep water, to stiffen the stems. The Dutch used special tulip vases, with holes along the top, one for each flower, or narrow, fan-shaped vases. Many people prefer to work with the character of a flower, rather than against it, allowing the stems to twist and curve at will. Using tall containers is an easy form of stem control, as is using a narrow-necked container or shortening the stem.

Hyacinths are popular as forced pot plants; as florists' flowers, they are much more expensive per stem than tulips and daffodils. Either way, hyacinths usually look better massed than singly. The densely packed flower spikes are heavy rather than graceful; it is as exquisite texture and colour, rather than as a form, that they excel. Hyacinths planted in the garden eventually become naturalized and revert to the wild, producing smaller flowers on less dense spikes.

Polyanthus, auriculas and pansies have intense 'faces', and posies of a single type are always pleasing. In his classic book, *The English Flower Garden* (1883), William Robinson wrote about flower arranging: 'One advantage of dealing with one flower at a time is that we show and do not conceal the variety of beauty we have.' Gertrude Jekyll also wrote that displaying flowers, of any type, on their own was inherently pleasing. Defining the difference between a charming display of single-species flowers and an anonymous, 'lifestyle'-type display is difficult. It is partly to do with the choice of container and setting; if an entire room looks as if it has been lifted straight from a furniture showroom or catalogue, a tall glass tumbler of daffodils absorbs some of that cool anonymity. That same tumbler of daffodils casually perched on the cluttered desk of a lived-in room can absorb and reflect a more personal, human – even humane – feeling. Knowing who created the display also colours

hite anemones and white cow
parsley are placed in a white setting
(above), and the display enlarged to include
white-flowered florists' *Euphorbia fulgens;*
Helichrysum petiolatum and tiny pink *Helleborus*.
Displays of single species flowers are always
aesthetically 'safe' and pleasing; whether they are
satisfactory on other levels depends very much on
their container, immediate propping, larger setting
and perhaps, ultimately, on the arranger!

35

perception of flowers, and whether they are there to be admired for their own beauty or 'posed' on behalf of the glory and good taste of their arranger.

On a practical level, the more polyanthus, auriculas and pansies are picked for massed displays, the more flower buds they produce, so generously full displays perpetuate themselves. Pansies are even more front-facing than daffodils. Seen from the side, they offer nothing, and a good approach is to present them like faces in a tiered auditorium, for observation and comparison.

Polyanthus and auriculas, and the related primroses and cowslips, are more three-dimensional, and mix easily with other small flowers, for example grape hyacinths, scillas, double daisies and pulmonarias. With small-scale mixed displays, uneven-length stalks help dispel formality, the flowers and their foliage settling naturally into a rounded mass, as if freshly gathered by hand from the garden and, indeed, they can be arranged in the hand to achieve just this effect.

Freesias used to be florists' spring flowers, but are now available all year round. They are usually sold in packets of five stems, which always look lonely on their own and need the company of branches or foliage, such as eucalyptus, pussy willow twigs, hazel twigs, young fringecup (*Tellima grandiflora*) or epimedium leaves, even parsley. Not all flowers are best accompanied by their own leaves: freesia leaves are long, floppy and unmemorable.

Hardy annuals sown in autumn begin to flower in late spring: sweet peas, godetia and cornflowers, or bachelor's buttons, love-in-a-mist and stocks.

SPRING SCENT

Many spring flowers have delightful scents. Early crocuses and irises have a light, fresh scent, best enjoyed at close range. Primroses, broom and *Tazetta* narcissi have a full but slightly astringent fragrance; that of lily of the valley, lilac, philadelphus, honeysuckle, hyacinth and *Azalea mollis* is more penetratingly sweet.

The violet is elusively scented. The Victorian method of capturing its fragrance indoors was to display cut violets in a glass-lidded bowl, with their stems pushed into damp silver sand. When scent was wanted, the lid was lifted momentarily. The glass cover also kept the humidity high, like a wardian case, and extended the life of the cut flowers inside. Being isolated within a glass case, though, made the flowers into a sort of museum exhibit, at one remove from direct contact.

Alliums, or ornamental onions, are largely spring flowering. Most emit their onion scent only when handled or bruised, so there should be no problem once a display is safely in position. The scent of crown imperials is also slightly musty but, again, is strongest when the plant is handled or bruised. Elderflower and thorn have heavy scents, which some people find unpleasant, but it may be that their association with high pollen counts and hay-fever partially colour perception.

A fragrant spring composition of periwinkle, lemon-scented tazetta narcissus, pink viburnum and tender jasmine, *Jasminum polyanthum* in flower, has a garland of ivy for good measure. Periwinkle, because it never produces sheets of colour, is often underrated in the garden, but its blue is beautifully clear, untouched by any hint of red. A painted rococo screen could add an element of romance to a bowl of cornflakes; here, as a bit of artistic licence, it reinforces the wistful, 'feminine' quality of the display.

Hyacinths and polyanthus are displayed with Spanish onions, plums and a scallop shell, on an American blue antique table. Hyacinth, in ancient mythology, was a beautiful youth, accidentally slain in a discus-throwing contest with his friend Apollo. Where Hyacinth's blood stained the ground, an exquisite flower sprang up; the grieving Apollo marked each petal with the letters of the Greek word meaning 'alas'. On a more mundane level, flowering forced hyacinth bulbs grow lanky with age, so cutting the flowers and displaying them in a tall container is a nice solution.

SPRING FOLIAGE

Autumn is the season associated with brilliantly coloured foliage, but spring also offers a good selection. Some young evergreen leaves, such as those of *Pieris*, *Camellia* and *Photinia* species, are bright orange, copper or crimson, gradually turning green as they age. Young whitebeam foliage is a beautiful downy white, and particularly attractive when its leaves are folded, showing the undersides. The *Acer* genus has many species and cultivars with softly coloured young foliage: *A. pseudoplatanus* 'Brillinatissimum', for example, with apricot-coloured young leaves; and *A. palmatum* 'Corallinum', with clear, shrimp-pink young leaves. The purple plum, *Prunus cerasifera* 'Pissardi', provides purple foliage, often nicer indoors than out, where it can appear crude, especially if close to laburnum.

Small, young oak leaves, although out relatively late in the season, are a delicate, fresh yellow-green, lovely with bluebells, paeonies or early roses. Like oak, unfolding horse-chestnut leaves have a delicacy absent from the mature foliage; cut and brought indoors in bud, they are a pleasure to observe over several days. Young spring foliage needs careful conditioning, and is relatively short-lived in any case, but enjoyable while it lasts.

Euphorbia foliage is useful in spring: the flower-like rosettes of *E. robbiae*; the oddly architectural spikes of caper spurge, *E. lathyris*; and the tall columns of grey-green *E. wulfenii*.

Unripe green honesty seed pods are leaf-like in shape, and sometimes stained with wine-red. Though less often used at this stage than when silvery and translucent, they are lovely with paeonies, tulips and lilac.

Some spring flowers – pansies, snowdrops, lilies of the valley, primroses, daffodils, snake's-head fritillaries – are well partnered with foliage, and an outer ruff or central column of their own leaves completes an indoor display. Substituting a flower's own leaves for different ones becomes an easy option from mid-spring onwards. Bearded irises, for example, have inflexibly upright foliage which is difficult to accommodate in a container. Substituting the more graceful leaves of *Iris sibirica*, or those of the yellow water iris, *I. pseudacorus*, creates a better result. Violet leaves with ranunculus, artichoke foliage with poppies, and hosta leaves with ranunculus and paeonies are all good combinations. Solomon's seal defies categorizing; its small hanging white flowers are charming, but its arching stalks and orderly pairs of leaves are its main attraction. The fountain-like growth habit lends itself to upright displays, on its own *en masse*, or surrounded by an outer ring of shorter material.

SPRING BRANCHES

As spring progresses the scale of cut-flower displays grows larger, and flowering branches can be as large as pruning allows. Species forced in winter can be brought indoors in spring to flower closer to their natural timing: chaenomeles, lilac and forsythia, snowy mespilus, Judas tree, philadelphus, quelder rose (*Viburnum opulus*) and spring-flowering viburnums.

An old-fashioned glass battery tank, filled with water-washed pebbles, seashells and water, holds fresh young larch branches. Larch is unusual among conifers in being deciduous, and usually has a graceful habit of growth, with downward-sweeping branches turning up at the ends. Here, they hide the leafless stem of a late-flowering hippeastrum. Bluebells, fragrant and archetypal spring flowers, look best by themselves, presented in a container that supports their stems. Ideally, cut, don't pull, the stems above the lower white stalks, to allow the bulb to build up strength for the following year.

A stuffed, black-throated diver seems bemused by the goose eggs nearby. Its colours are repeated in the lotus seed pods, pussy willow and contorted willow branches, seemingly standing of their own accord in clear glass containers. Willow plants are either male or female; male plants produce the soft, fluffy catkins, or pussies, while the female flowers are modest. Shrubby species tend to produce better catkins than tree species; the name 'pussy willow' refers specifically to the male form of *Salix caprea* or goat willow.

rape hyacinths inserted into the dense, flat heads of florists' trachelium, which acts visually as foliage. White sea sponge and annual sea lavender, or statice, provide textural accompaniment. As well as grape hyacinth's own grassy leaves, bergenia, ivy, periwinkle or dead nettle foliage could be substituted from the garden; from the house, a few sprigs of tradescantia or large African violet leaves would do nicely.

Magnolia is slow-growing and pruning has to be restrained, but cut branches in flower need no other accompaniment. Branches of fruit-tree blossom and ornamental fruit trees – flowering almond, crab apple, cherry and plum – and blackthorn branches, cut in bud, make dramatic indoor displays. The cut branches of azalea in blossom, especially the soft colours of the deciduous types, are easy to display indoors, and can range in scale from a single twiggy blossom in a bud vase to several large branches.

Large-flowered rhododendrons are more difficult, ironically, since to many people they are the apotheosis of spring beauty. The size of the flower-heads dictates large-scale displays, unless the truss is dismembered and the florets floated in water. Because they have awkwardly shaped branches, and the bare branch between one set of flowers and leaves and the next lacks the linear grace of, say, magnolia, large-flowered rhododendrons do not mix easily with other flowers. A traditional approach is to tightly mass the leafless rhododendron flower heads in a huge mound of colour, like enormous scoops of raspberry sherbert. To some people this is breathtaking, to others a classic example of 'too much of a good thing'.

SPRING INSPIRATIONS, OBSERVATIONS AND PROJECTS

• Observe the growth habit of flowering shrubs and trees, before cutting material for an indoor display. Try to retain their angle of growth in the display: upright for lilacs, arching outwards and downwards for broom, horizontal for *Viburnum plicatum* 'Mariesii', and so on.

• Place cut flowering branches in a broad, shallow container and surround the base of the branches with fresh moss. Again, try to retain the branches' natural growth habit. Use florists' foam block, metal pin-holders or compressed wire mesh netting for support. With heavy Japanese pin-holders, beautiful in their own right,

According to the Victorian 'Language of Flowers', forget-me-nots stood for true love and constancy, and often appeared on Valentine cards as well as the occasional Christmas card. Their Latin name, *Myosotis*, comes from the Greek *mys*, meaning mouse, and *otis*, meaning ear, and refers to the shape of the leaves. As cut flowers, forget-me-nots displayed on their own have an innocent charm; used with other flowers, they act like gypsophila, creating a soft blue haze.

replace the moss with water, for a miniature waterscape. In keeping with the Oriental philosophy of flower arranging, display water-loving plants such as sprigs or branches of alder, willow, arum, variegated sweet flag, hosta or water iris, on pinholders in shallow, water-filled dishes.

Observe and draw the changing shape of tulip or ranunculus stems in a container over the course of several days.

Dig up large clumps of polyanthus, auriculas, primroses and cowslips in bud, transfer them to a lined wicker basket or large bowl, cover the root-ball with a thick layer of moss and display them in a cool room indoors. When flowering is over, divide the clumps, to keep them healthy, and replant in the garden.

Display hanging, bell-shaped flowers such as crown imperials high enough to be seen from below. Display tiny spring flowers such as forget-me-nots and primroses low enough to be seen from above. Display short-stemmed flowers such as aubrieta and primulas in tight bands or patterns of colour, like a parterre or knot garden of flowers.

Mix wild spring flowers such as elder blossom and cow parsley or Queen Anne's lace with florists' flowers.

When spring pruning houseplants with attractive leaves, such

45

as zonal, ivy-leaved and scented pelargoniums, use the cuttings as foliage for small flowers such as double daisies, grape hyacinths and auriculas.

● Study seventeenth-century Flemish flower paintings of idealized mixed bunches of spring flowers, observing the props and backdrops.

● Study the colour variation in pansies, auriculas and bicolour tulips. Using watercolours or coloured pencils, design imaginary colour combinations.

● Buy carpet samples to use as 'sets' for cut-flower displays. Collect samples of top-quality floral-printed fabric, such as Liberty cottons and William Morris patterns, to use as inspirations, backdrops or foregrounds for spring displays.

● Collect old crochet-work, lace and open-weave curtains and offcuts. Experiment with the shadows they cast and how they filter light. Draw the shadows. Overlay printed fabric with open-weave fabric, noting the changing patterns as one slightly moves in relation to the other.

SPRING TIPS

● A few drops of bleach in vase water helps keep wallflowers, rhododendrons and stocks fresh, and helps prevent alliums smelling of onions.

● Cut wallflower stems short, and give the flowers a long drink in warm water before arranging them.

● Dip cut epimediums, broom, spiraea and elderflower stems briefly in boiling water before giving them a long drink. Treat cut polyanthus, ranunculus and auricula stems in the same way, but also prick their stems just under the flower heads to release trapped air and allow water to be taken up freely.

● Condition woody branches of young spring foliage, as well as rhododendron, magnolia, laburnum, lilac and philadelphus, by hammering the cut ends before giving them a long drink in warm water. Defoliate philadelphus, lilac and laburnum to prevent premature wilting.

● Dip cut clematis flower stalks briefly in boiling water, then completely submerge the flowers for an hour or two before displaying them. Dip cut wisteria stalks briefly in alcohol, then place them in a deep container of water for several hours. Neither of these flowers is long-lasting when cut, but will manage for at least an evening, if conditioned.

● Leave cut arum lilies in a deep container, filled with water up to the base of the flowers, for several hours before displaying them.

● To refresh violets, submerge them completely overnight, and rearrange them the next morning.

● Tulips and arum lilies are heavy drinkers; re-cut the stems and check the water regularly.

● Keep freesias, irises, sweet William, stock and broom away from wilting flowers, ripening fruit and vegetables, which release harmful ethylene gas; and out of heat, draughts and direct sunlight.

Pot et fleur conventionally refers to cut flowers and pot plants displayed within a single container. In the broader sense, it can simply mean their close juxtaposition, as in this spring-garden-on-a-table. White hippeastrums provide support and company for each other; *en masse*, the awkwardness of single stems is eliminated. Clivia's strappy leaves are sufficient accompaniment for its flowers; sphagnum moss hides the compost, retains moisture and creates a tiny lawn. The potted polyanthus can be bought in flower and later planted outdoors, or potted up from the garden while in bud, then returned to the garden afterwards.

*Y*ellow and red parrot tulips, pyracantha blossom, laburnum and spring turnips are shown with a patterned cloth used horizontally and vertically, as foreground and background, a standard photography practice. Its painterly daubs of colour suggests possible flower combinations; another alternative is shown on page 18. Though photographed with its leaves, cut laburnum flowers (like those of lilac) are longer-lasting if defoliated.

ichaelmas daises, *Nicotiana*,
delphiniums, geraniums, lupins,
pelargoniums, China asters and
Euphorbia wulfenii overspill an old-fashioned
wicker trug. While this arrangement captures the
variety of form and red-and-pink theme of summer
flowers, heaping cut flowers in this way is liable to
damage them, and the stems should be placed in
water as soon as possible.

SUMMER

I loved the violet and lily of the valley, but above all, the rose
– all roses, and we had many sorts, damask, cabbage,
'Scotch', moss, and white roses in multitude on a great shady
bush that overhung the little street at our garden-foot. The
profusion of these warm-scented white roses gave a great
feeling of summer wealth and joy, but my constant favourite
was the 'Monthly Rose', in colour and fragrance the acme of
sweetness and delicacy combined, and keeping up, even in
winter time, its faithful and delicate companionship.

A Diary, WILLIAM ALLINGHAM, 1824–89

White florists' roses are combined with pyracantha, or firethorn, in bloom. Better known and more often grown for its orange, red or yellow berries, pyracantha is closely related to cotoneaster and produces fluffy masses of hawthorn-like scented white flowers in May and June. Blackbirds and sparrows love the berries, but any that escape the birds and the rigours of annual pruning look lovely with autumn dahlias and chrysanthemums.

Late spring is often so pleasant that the advent of summer can go unnoticed. It officially begins on 21 June, the summer solstice, the longest day of the year when the sun is overhead at the tropic of Cancer. In England, the start of summer is confusingly called 'midsummer'; parties are traditionally held on Midsummer's Day, 24 June, taking advantage of the long, light evening and the frivolity associated with midsummer madness.

For children, the start of summer is marked by the end of the school year, early in June for American children and as late as mid-July for the long-suffering English. For many American children, summer nights mean catching fireflies, or 'lightning bugs' as they are more prosaically called; and picking off huge bronzy-green Japanese beetles from rose bushes during the day. For English children,

I n the Victorian 'Language of Flowers',
an elaborate system of communication for
courting couples, the scarlet poppy
symbolized 'fantastic extravagance', perhaps
because of its short but brilliant life. To the red-blind
honeybees that pollinate poppies, the scarlet colour
reflects ultraviolet, enabling the flowers to be seen
and visited, and the dark central blotch on each petal
advertises the proximity of pollen.

summer may mean summer pudding, an exquisite concoction of bread and stewed raspberries and redcurrants, or fresh strawberries and cream dusted with icing sugar. For ardent fishermen on both sides of the Atlantic, summer begins in mid-June with the start of the coarse fishing season, after three months' restraint.

To many, the last frost marks the start of summer and the planting out of geraniums, fuchsias and petunias, but vestiges of spring remain for some time afterwards, in overblown tulips, wall-flowers and even a few late daffodils. In the wild, the elderflower, with its sickly-sweet fragrance, continues into early summer, together with the more elusive scent of the dog rose (*Rosa canina*), perhaps mingling with the heavier fragance of lily of the valley.

Summer provides a surfeit of flowers: irises, paeonies, sweet peas, carnations, delphiniums, scabious, love-in-a-mist, violets, nasturtium, lilies and day lilies, lupins, stocks, poppies and, above all, roses. Later, gladioli, China asters, Michaelmas daisies, dahlias, red-hot pokers and early chrysanthemums help late summer slip into autumn.

For those without gardens, summer means cheap cut flowers, especially annuals, and the potential for creating relaxed, seemingly home-grown displays as opposed to florists' ones. For those with gardens, it means every free minute spent outdoors, working or just sitting out. However splendid a garden, bringing cut flowers indoors is still worthwhile, not only for the pleasure of the display but because summer storms can ruin the perfection of fragile flowers such as irises, and because many flowers, such as roses, sweet peas and Shirley poppies, produce more the more they are cut. And within the confines of a room, a particular floral fragrance becomes more intense and can therefore be more fully enjoyed.

Summer lacks the anticipatory quality of spring, and also the slightly reminiscent quality of autumn. Summer is an intense daily thrill, derived entirely from the present.

SUMMER COLOURS

There is a surfeit of colour in summer, too, compared to winter's predominant blacks, greys and whites, spring's pastel tints or autumn's brilliant oranges and subtle browns. In cool temperate climates, much of summer's brilliant polychromatic palette comes from half-hardy and tender annuals: zinnia, cosmos, marigold, ageratum and dahlia from Mexico; petunia, salvia, verbena and tobacco plant from South America; busy Lizzie from Zanzibar; and pelargonium and lobelia from South Africa. These intensely bright colours, so suited to hot, brilliant light, were much loved by the Victorians. They devised endless bedding-out schemes in geometric patterns of riveting colour, and had the cheap garden labour and greenhouse heating necessary to provide huge numbers of bedding-out plants annually to meet the demand.

Bedding began to fall out of favour after 1883, when William Robinson, an influential Victorian gardener, wrote his classic book *The English Flower Garden*, praising the informal cottage garden.

The sunflower, a typical member of the *Compositae* family, contains up to 2000 florets per flower head; its nectar is much sought after by insects, especially honeybees. As cut and garden flowers, their bright-yellow, sunny colour and open, simple 'faces' make them endearing to children and adults alike. Stunning on their own or, as here, with coreopsis, daisy and helianthus, they can also be displayed with huge branches of autumn foliage or berries. To make cut sunflowers last, dip the cut ends in boiling water for a few seconds, then give them a long, cool drink.

Two and three-dimensional flowers fill this *tableau vivant*: floral motifs are woven into the table carpet backdrop and foreground fabric, and more flowers appear on the jugs, mugs and punchbowl. From the left, carved wooden roses around the punchbowl rim mingle with fresh chrysanthemums and roses; wooden roses encircle the pink china asters and the single, bronze-red spray chrysanthemums; and a cluster of blue gentians and poppies complete this polychromatic display. The scattered petals and pink mallow florets are artistic licence, but would remain fresh long enough to make a good arrangement for a drinks or dinner party.

Later, Gertrude Jekyll and Vita Sackville West, English gardeners and writers, continued to promote the style of natural-looking, informal plantings and drifts of intermingling colour, inspired by the natural distribution of plants in a woodland or meadow.

Nonetheless, bedding out has remained popular, and will no doubt continue to be so because of the instant gratification of being able to go to a garden centre, buy plants in flower and have the colour *in situ* all in the space of an hour. Then, too, dealing formally with identical plants of identical height, form and colour is reassuring to many people, and the straight rows and simple geometric patterns make minimal demands on creativity.

What purists find so disconcerting and unsettling about bedding out in general, and modern bedding plants in particular, is the proportion of flower to leaf and stem or, in another way of putting it, non-green to green. Though seed catalogues proudly proclaim of a new F1 hybrid, 'so free-flowering that not a leaf is in sight', a living

Roses and peaches encapsulate the glorious range of pinks available from the summer garden. The cultivars photographed include the bright-pink floribunda 'Romance', climbing rose 'Golden Showers', the pale-pink 'Queen Elizabeth' and the cerise 'Blue Parfum'. The frilly quality of the rose petals is echoed by the frilly Victorian glass fruit stand.

plant struggling to support flowers in excess of what is natural looks uncomfortable, like a skinny person trying to carry a huge one. Even early on, the discerning few noticed the unnaturalness; in *Potpourri from a Surrey Garden* (1912) Mrs C. W. Earle wrote:

> *... but I warn everyone against those terrible*
> *inventions of the seedsmen, dwarf*
> *Antirrhinums, they have all the attributes of a*
> *dwarf and are impish and ugly. The flower is*
> *far too large for the stalk, and they are, to my*
> *mind, entirely without merit.*

Visiting the Royal Horticultural Society's annual Chelsea Show is another summer lesson in large-scale floral colour. Tightly packed stands, displaying hundreds of delphiniums, roses, paeonies, tulips or clematis, attest to growers' skills, but discourage the appreciation of a particular flower's colour, form or fragrance. Like a museum with too many Renoirs in the same room, a floral display with too many flowers can be overwhelming, even crude, and quickly tire the eye's ability to appreciate it.

Just as the rose dominates the summer garden, its colours dominate the floral palette. With the exception of cool whites such as the Floribunda 'Iceberg' and curious silvery mauves such as the hybrid tea 'Blue Moon', roses have warm colours, with reds and pinks predominating. Paeonies, phlox, carnations, sweet peas and poppies, archetypal summer flowers, together with rhododendrons, which span spring and summer, reinforce this red and pink seasonal theme. The different colours attract specific pollinators: red flowers attract swallowtail butterflies, for example.

Red is a colour of many moods and aspects, some curiously contradictory. Red, and its tint, pink, have decidedly 'feminine' overtones. Red is the colour of Valentine cards, of the roses that profess love and devotion; and the Red Cross and Red Crescent are symbols of mercy. Red ribbons and rosettes are for winners; 'red-letter days' are especially successful, memorable ones. Red can also intimate power; 'red-blooded', for example, means vigorous, even virile; and 'red-carpet' treatment is given only to the powerful. Red also has sexual connotations, with references to 'red-light districts', for example, or a 'scarlet woman'. It is an aggressive colour, and red cars are often associated with aggressive driving. To 'see red' is to become enraged; to 'wave a red rag' is to enrage someone else. Red road signs warn of danger, and red lights mean 'stop'. To be caught 'red handed', or to have a bank balance 'in the red' is no good. The devil is traditionally garbed in red, Hell is red hot, and even bureaucracy, a contemporary manifestation of Hell, is symbolized by red tape.

Pink is more lighthearted, perhaps in keeping with its higher light content, and pink champagne, pink gin, pink elephants and a pink negligée all symbolize frivolity. 'In the pink' means in the best of health, although pink flowers actually have a certain fragility, bruising and discolouring easily.

The psychology of colour affects the appreciation of flowers, but their positive and peaceful connotations tend to override the fierce or negative emotive values of red. The red used in a danger sign attracts and holds the eye when seen in a rose, but does not intimidate. One exception, perhaps, is red gladiolus, whose generic name comes, tellingly, from the Latin for 'sword'. The fiercely erect, unbendable stem, sword-like leaves and massive flowers, especially when red, do have a challenging, almost military presence. So, too, does *Strelitzia reginae*, the bird of paradise flower; though more orange than red, to some its fiercely predatory-looking, beak-like flower bract appears almost intimidating.

Red's closest neighbours are orange and violet. A scarlet red that veers towards orange is much brighter and more luminous than a crimson red that contains violet. Crimsons tend to be sombre and sober, intimating nobility, wealth, stability, wisdom, perhaps even 'old' money. Scarlet embodies the youthful, more casual side of red: plastic shop-front fascias in shopping malls are more likely to be orange-red than blue-red.

In a cut-flower display, as in the garden, crimson flowers are visually recessive, creating 'holes' like dark entrances to caves, especially if seen against paler foliage and flowers and lit from behind. Lit from the front, crimson flowers, especially those with velvet-textured petals, can be intensely beautiful, inviting the eye to explore their depths. (This velvet texture, so exquisite to the human sensibility, is simply another aid to pollination. The outer layer of petal cells, which normally form a smooth, flat surface, instead bulge out so that each cell forms a microscopic hill, creating a light trap and colour pattern attractive to pollinating insects.) Pink flowers, because of their luminosity, stand out visually and appear less massive than a similar flower in crimson tones. Huge pale-pink double paeonies, for example, have the lightness of a ballet tutu,

ose thorns are annoying, but in
nature help the plant make its way
through adjacent branches to reach
the sun, and protect it from foraging animals. Like
colour, thorns vary from one species to another.
Rosa laevigata, the cherokee rose, for example, has
hooked thorns on its calyx; *R. sericea ptericantha*
has fiercely sharp, translucent crimson thorns; and
the Bourbon rose 'Zephirine Drouhan' is thornless.
Use a sharp knife or disposable razor to dethorn
roses, as part of conditioning.

whereas huge crimson double paeonies convey a sense of weightiness. Pinks can appear subtle, delicate or insipid, according to the surrounding colours and the style of the display. Scale is also important: large-flowered gladioli in coppery pink are reminiscent of cheap nylon lingerie; that same colour in smaller, fragile poppies is enchanting.

As with red, there is no one pink, and referring to pink flowers is referring to a whole spectrum of tints. Gertrude Jekyll, in *Home and Garden* (1900), wrote:

> *It is very easy to say pink, but pink covers such a wide range, from warm ash colour to pale salmon red, and from the tint of a new-born mushroom to that of an ancient brick. One might prepare a range of at least thirty tints – and this number could easily be multiplied – all of which might be called pink; yet with regard to some room or object or flower of any one kind of red, only a few of these will be in friendly accordance, a good number will be in deadly discord, and the remainder more or less out of relation.*

To avoid confusion in the construction and interior design industries, British Standards developed a system of numbering thousands of specific paint colours, many of which also have 'common names': blush pink, for example, and dusky pink. The American Rose Society has officially adopted 16 colours to describe rose varieties: white or near white; medium yellow; deep yellow; yellow blend; apricot blend; orange and orange blend; orange-red; light pink; medium pink; deep pink; pink blend; medium red; dark red; red blend; russet and mauve. Even so, that numbered or named colour will almost certainly appear different in natural and artificial light, and different again in incandescent and fluorescent light, and in warm- or cool-toned light. Then too, tiny sample squares of colour can give a false impression of that same tone covering an entire wall.

Numbering specific or varietal flower colours in the same way, both for accurate description and the creation of foolproof floral display recipes – so that one could say, for example, that numbers 6 and 27 go well together, but 4 and 27 do not – would not work for other reasons, as well as those given for paint colours (it also demeans flowers, and reduces them to the level of hurried, late-night orders in a take-away restaurant). Many flowers, especially roses, change colour, usually fading, as they age. The Gallica rose 'Cardinal de Richelieu', for example, is dark purple when young, fading to Parma violet. China roses deepen in colour with age. The orange-red buds of *R. chinensis* 'Mutabilis' open into single, fragrant yellow flowers, turn coppery pink and, finally, coppery red. The modern Floribunda 'Masquerade' does likewise – the effect, especially when seen *en masse*, can be described as stunning and spectacular or

collection of modest floral jugs and
summer florists' flowers, each
'propping' the other. From the left, violets
with their leaves; pink Turk's-cap ranunculus; pink
anemones, with a single purple outrider, and blue
trachelium and white Brompton stock, cow parsley
and pink lisianthus. Photographed against a mossy
wooden wall, the flowers automatically derive
informality from their setting, and from the resting
bunch of ranunculus, looking as if it is about to be
placed in water.

bizarre and garish, depending on taste. Remontant roses often carry a different-coloured rose in late summer or autumn from the main, early summer display.

The pink flower buds of *Pulmonaria officinalis*, or lungwort, open into blue flowers, hence its other common name, soldiers and sailors. And the so-called changing forget-me-not, *Myosotis versicolor*, unfurls yellow, then fades through pink to blue. All these colour changes are thought to be pre- and post-pollination signals to insects, informing them of the flowers to visit, for their mutual benefit.

Some cut flowers, such as sweet peas, open paler when picked in bud than when picked fully open. Some flowers change colour in sunlight or hot weather: the Bourbon rose 'Mme Pierre Oger', for example, is silvery pink, but deep rose-pink in sunlight and during hot summers. The white-flowered Hortensia, or mophead, hydrangea, 'Mme Emile Mouillière', matures to a rich pink in full sun but is green in shade. Mophead hydrangeas are also famous, or infamous, for having flower colours responding to soil acidity, being blue in acid soil and pink in neutral or alkaline soil. (Cottagers once buried iron nails when planting hydrangeas to ensure blue flowers even in neutral or alkaline soil; today, regular applications of sequestered iron may be given.)

Not only are flower-colour descriptions inadequate, but so are giving exact colour recipes, since choice of colours must always be subjective. Many people find pinks or reds tinged with yellow, combined with pinks or reds tinged with blue, startling, but other people do not. Then, too, as rose stamens are yellow, excluding yellow from displays of violet-tinged pink roses (especially single and semi-double roses) is not a realistic option.

SUMMER FRAGRANCE AND SHAPES

Fragrance is a particular summer treat, with so many scented flowers in bloom, including roses, stocks, border carnations, lavender, mignonette, heliotrope, sweet peas, scented geranium and jasmine. Roses themselves have a huge range of fragrance, both heavy and subtle: *Rosa banksiae*, for example, smells of violets, the burnet rose smells of lily of the valley, and *Rosa rugosa* 'Rosairie de l'Hay' smells of sugared almonds. There are roses smelling of cloves, lemons, apples, nasturtiums, orris, myrrh, apricots, raspberries and even bananas (the last comes from the late-flowering creamy-white climber *Rosa longicuspis*).

Fragrance, like colour, attracts pollinating insects: the lovely night scent of tobacco plants, night-scented stocks and daturas acts as a beacon to night-flying moths. Petunias and jasmine smell strongest in the evenings and at night; Darwin observed that white was the dominant colour of fragrant flowers, because white can most easily be seen at night.

Summer fragrance comes from leaves as well: herbs, of course, especially mints; artemisias; and scented-leaved pelargoniums, smelling of roses, nutmeg, lemon, orange or peppermint, according to variety. The leaves of *Rosa primula* are said to smell of incense.

*S*ea lavender, astilbe, lavender and cherries appear in a frothy still life with old metal kitchen implements. Lavender and sea lavender are excellent subjects for creating a still life; unlike many fresh flowers, they remain intact and turgid out of water, and eventually dry of their own accord. Astilbes are rather the opposite, and must have their cut ends seared or dipped in boiling water, otherwise they wilt, even in water.

A table full of summer imagery and
fragrance: jasmine, sweet Williams,
sweet peas, pinks, regal pelargonium
and strawberries. Summer jasmine is short lived as a
cut flower, but dipping the cut end briefly in boiling
water, followed by a long drink, maximizes its life.
Regal pelargoniums are longer lasting when cut than
zonal, or bedding, pelargoniums; use them in small-
scale posies, perhaps with scented geranium foliage.

isplaying a plant in flower, with its
fruit nearby, is an approach that can
easily be taken with strawberries in
season, but even a bed of the appropriate leaves can
create a refreshing, just-picked impression. Try
serving a bunch of grapes on a bed of grape leaves, or
currants on a bed of currant leaves. You can 'cheat'
in both cases if necessary, using foliage from
ornamental vines or ornamental flowering currants.

*B*rompton stock and cow parsley are combined in a study of whites and greens. Though florists' flowers are used, the effect is one of gardens and hedgerows, partly because of the informal 'garden bunch' style and the Tudor whitewashed and oak-beam backdrop. A drop or two of bleach in the water helps prevent Brompton stocks and other members of the *Cruciferae* family fouling the water.

Though the vast majority of leaf scents are attractive to the human nose, they act, in nature, as deterrents to herbivorous animals and insects. The 'cottage-garden' system of companion planting – French or African marigolds planted next to tomatoes, for example, to deter whitefly – is based on this natural defence system, which has none of the harmful side-effects associated with chemical pesticides.

Even flower shapes are invitations to specific insect pollinators. In temperate climates, most flowers are pollinated by bees, insects which prefer elongated flowers with little landing pads from which to probe for pollen. Many flowers, in the interests of survival, oblige them: the vast *Labiatae* family, with their lip-shaped lower petals, such as dead-nettles, bells of Ireland, sage, hyssop, rosemary, cat-mint; and the *Scrophulariaceae* family, with their large, lipped or pouched lower petals, including foxgloves, snapdragons, cal-ceolaria, penstemons, toadflax, mimulus, mulleins and speedwells.

Summer is also the season for the *Umbelliferae* family, which includes cow parsley, Queen Anne's lace, sea holly, astrantia, dill, fennel and angelica. Their large, flat or rounded landing pads accommodate many types of pollinating insects, including flies, beetles and occasionally butterflies. Flat flowers and those with big

Some species of eucalyptus have the lovely, irregular and unruly quality of garden foliage, and are ideal for combining with obvious florists' flowers, such as hybrid roses and iris. Artichoke leaves are beautiful, but are sometimes unreliable as cut foliage. Choose mature leaves, and dip the cut stalks in boiling water for a few seconds, then submerge the leaves in cold water for at least an hour.

central discs, such as daisies and scabious, viburnums and elderberry, also welcome virtually all comers.

Grasses, both ornamental long grasses and closely cropped lawns, are summer features, and the elusive scent of a new-mown lawn is as important an evocation of the season as more seductive fragrances. Because the flowers of the *Gramineae* family are largely wind-pollinated, no effort is made to please the insect eye: flowers are small, insignificant and green or beigy-brown in colour. In cut-flower displays, the modesty and delicacy of ornamental wild grasses – quaking grass, oat grass, Bowles' golden grass, foxtail, cloud grass and hare's tail grass – are excellent for offsetting dense masses of floral colour. Even the relatively crude plumes of pampas grass can be taken apart into feathery, delicate portions, for visually softening ordinary-sized displays.

SUMMER FOLIAGE

In the garden, green is taken for granted, and its valuable job of separating other colours from one another, and providing restful areas for the eye, is overlooked. Foliage gardens are said to 'lack colour', and the proverbial 'riot of colour' in seed catalogues never refers to green. The value of foliage – almost any foliage – becomes immediately obvious when one buys cut flowers, and possible display ideas take shape in the mind's eye.

If gardening combines nature and art in equal parts, displaying cut flowers might be said to be two parts art to one part nature. The proportions of greenery to flower can either mimic nature or go against it, with some or even all leaves removed. It is often easier to create an attractive cut-flower display from the garden than from florists' flowers, many of which are defoliated before being sold, and present uniformly straight and uninteresting stems. Garden flowers often have, as well as their own foliage, imperfect stems that give character to a display – a slight twist, crookedness or branching. Garden flowers are also less likely to be disbudded, so that a single branch may have flowers, albeit smaller than those from a florist, in various stages of maturity.

Looking at a mass of brilliant, contrasting flower colour unrelieved by green can excite but also quickly tire the eye; whether that is the effect wanted is a personal choice. A mass of harmonious colour – say, from pale ivory pink to deep rose – unrelieved by green is more soothing than exciting, and also less tiring, but it could be considered unadventurous – again, this is a subjective response.

In the colour wheel, green is opposite red, its complementary colour. Pure, flat red and pure, flat green vibrate when in juxtaposition. Fortunately, nothing in the garden is chromatically pure or flat, like a piece of coloured paper. Rose foliage alone ranges from matt to glossy, and from the bright, apple-green of *Rosa rugosa* to the purple-tinged blue grey of *Rosa rubrifolia*. Some matt, mid-green foliage – like that of philadelphus, lilac and weigela, for example – lacks memorable character, compared to glossier or more flamboyantly shaped green leaves such as those of camellia or *Fatsia japonica*. Nonetheless, these modest leaves provide green in bulk, as a setting for their flowers and, like a dull but loyal lover, are only missed when they are gone.

Summer is the season for silver and grey foliage, as welcome for cut-flower displays as in the garden. Equally effective with pastels and intense tones, silver foliage reflects light and softens fierce floral contrasts. *Senecio* 'Sunshine', an easy-going shrub previously known as *S. greyi* and *S. laxifolius*, is the most sensible choice for a steady supply of grey foliage for cut-flower displays. Though less brilliantly white or silver than, say, *S.* 'White Diamond' or *S.* 'Ramparts', it is evergreen, and presentable all year round. Its yellow, ragwort-type flowers should be nipped in the bud, otherwise the foliage tends to become dull and dark towards the end of summer; the buds themselves are like silver baubles, and worth including in cut-flower displays, or in containers on their own.

The huge *Artemisia* genus also provides a wealth of foliage, usually lacy or otherwise delicate, but only in summer and autumn; in spring the growth is too soft to remain rigid when cut, and quickly wilts. For massive displays, there is mullein (*Verbascum bombicyferum*) and giant thistle (*Onopordum arabicum*); their lower leaves

A well-planned garden can provide an infinite number of floral 'sets', such as this vignette of an old white-painted wrought-iron garden seat, set in the midst of trumpet and Asiatic hybrid lilies, delphiniums, tagetes and summer foliage. Carefully composed photographs of successful gardens in full bloom can provide inspiration for grouping cut flowers indoors.

can also be used in medium-sized and small displays.

One might think that foliage is varied in its beauty simply in order to please the eye – a philosophy popular in Victorian times, when it was also thought that moral lessons could be derived from natural phenomena – but the silvery hue is a survival mechanism. The fine hairs or waxy coating that reflect light also help reduce leaf transpiration in hot, dry weather; most silver and grey plants come from such climates. They are difficult to condition for use in cut-flower displays, but it can be done (see page 80).

Variegated foliage, on the other hand, serves no natural purpose, and its presence in gardens and garden centres is due to the human penchant for the unusual, combined with our ingenuity and intervention. Most variegated plants now cultivated originated as 'sports'. These are odd plants or even single branches with bizarrely different foliage from the species, as a result of genetic mutation, and are propagated vegetatively from cuttings, to retain the variegated characteristic. In the garden, they usually need cossetting, as varie-gated plants tend to be slower- and weaker-growing than their all-green counterparts. Variegated foliage, like a bedding plant, will always be popular because it is often showy, and in some cases – variegated New Zealand flax, for example – the colour is as striking as flower colour.

Variegated foliage ranges from the subtle to the discordant; using it in cut-flower displays involves using the same instincts towards colour and taste as with flowers. Handsome displays can be made with branches of variegated foliage alone; combining several different types of variegated foliage can look frenzied or like a *pointillist* painting, depending on the choice of material and one's subjective feelings.

SUMMER SETTINGS

A lovely landscape is the best possible backdrop for summer flowers: rolling countryside, the sea, fields or woodlands. Indoors, a bit of 'street wisdom' is called for, to achieve pleasing results. The idea of displaying a single flower such as a rosebud, unencumbered by other blossom, is a case in point; an example is shown on page 74. A photographer, within the frame of a picture, can be an absolute despot, rearranging objects within the square or rectangle of the finished image, and ruthlessly eliminating the paraphernalia and

*Y*ou can almost smell the farm in this rustic setting where outrageously bold late summer colours successfully fly in the face of traditional combinations. Cactus, semi-cactus, decorative and anemone-flowered dahlias in orange, red, yellow, pink and white are arranged colour by colour in a collection of old jugs. Stripped of their own leaves, the dahlias are 'cooled' by their setting of mossy brick and stonework.

A single flower can be a welcome relief from extravagant cut-flower displays, especially if chosen and 'propped' with care. Here, a rosebud is accompanied by old-fashioned pink glass sugar and salt shakers placed on an old piano. Equally important visually is the 'breathing space' surrounding the display. Single flowers can often be rescued when dismantling faded displays.

detritus of ordinary human life. He or she can also control absolutely the intensity, quality and direction of light, creating the feeling of a sunny summer afternoon in a windowless studio. The state of the art is such that moods can be created to match any brief, and the humblest subject, whether a simple flower or, as is often the case in food photography, a boiled egg or sliced beetroot, becomes an image far more powerful and grandiose than in real life.

In the home, displays of cut flowers usually have to take their chances with other domestic objects, and lose any grandiose quality they might at first possess rather quickly. Japanese followers of Ikebana solved this problem by setting aside a specially built wall niche for the display of flower arrangements. Called a *tokonoma*, it might contain a painted scroll depicting a landscape scene, together with bronze, porcelain or lacquer objects – incense burners, for example, or figures – considered especially beautiful and held in special esteem, irrespective of their monetary value. These 'props' helped set the mood for the creation of a flower display, and for its appreciation once it was finished. When a guest visited, he or she was given a special floral display, complete with flowers and objects, to observe and contemplate.

*A*nnual Iceland poppies show off their extreme fragility and beauty. The unruly stems become a feature in the clear glass tumbler, creating interesting spaces between them, and the subtle flower colours capture the warmth of late-summer light. The highly polished piano surface reflects the form and colour, a trick repeatable on a domestic scale with a silver or metal serving tray.

Since niches rarely form part of the domestic architecture of Western houses, a special effort has to be made to create sympathetic settings for flower displays. The most likely locations for cut flowers – coffee tables, end tables, dining tables, fireplace mantelpieces, bookshelves, and so on – may be approached with some of the attitude of a photographer setting up a shot. Unnecessary paraphernalia can be removed (even if just to another part of the room) and empty space (referred to as 'visual breathing space' or 'working white' in the trade) created. This can remain empty, or filled with suitably evocative fabric or other items, or even *objets trouvés*; the picture on page 58 is a good example.

With small displays, such as the single rosebud, proximity is everything: closeness allows observation, even a sort of communion, with the flower and its surrounding objects. Theoretically, a desk would be ideal, and images of executive desks, empty of all but flowers and a leather-framed family photograph, are perhaps an equivalent of the Japanese *tokonoma*. Even on muddled desks, a small container of flowers, or a single flower, can provide a resting place for the eye, and momentary diversion from the rest of life. (A stable container is of course vital.)

A late summer study in blue, white and green has large-flowered white gladioli in an Oriental vase and summer jasmine foliage, ceanothus blossom and silky clematis seed heads making a tiny posy in a smaller container in a happy relationship between light, lace, vases and flowers.

ool maritime colours dominate this little vignette of meticulously positioned shells and summer flowers of beheaded echinops, or globe thistle; and astrantia, or masterwort. Rows of similar attractive objects, such as the scallop shells shown, set up a pleasing rhythm, and the bleached blue wooden background is reminiscent of the sea.

SUMMER INSPIRATIONS, OBSERVATIONS AND PROJECTS

• Collect and carefully display one type of flower in all stages of growth: buds, newly open flowers, fully open blooms and seed pods or hips. Poppies are good for this, as are roses. With spikes of flowers, such as acanthus, delphiniums and foxgloves, observe the various stages of maturity within a single spike. The special beauty of ageing is a quality much appreciated in Ikebana; leave petals of spent cut roses where they fall, round the base of the display.

• Cut garden flowers to stems of different lengths and bunch them directly in the hand, evenly building up the outside of the bunch. Transfer the bunch as it is to a simple container, for a natural, graceful display with an interesting outline.

• When pruning trees and shrubs, take some of the prunings indoors, to display and perhaps to draw. Displaying branches also plays a major role in Ikebana – as important a role as flowers – and

single branches are studied as objects of great beauty.

  • Display flowers with their own foliage, and experiment with substituting other garden foliage. This exercise can help you see how a flower's colour and form alter according to their immediate surroundings. Try a row of little pots containing the same flower, each with different foliage.

  • Move a flower display from a south-facing window to a north-facing one, and note the difference in colour. Move it to artificial light, and look again; if you have both fluorescent and incandescent lights, study the effect each has on certain colours: reds and blues, for example. You can also collect freshly fallen petals, or those from over-mature flowers, and try different juxtapositions of colours, even for an hour or for an afternoon. Try juxtaposing petals on a plain surface, such as white formica; and a patterned surface, such as a tablecloth, scarf, or length of fabric.

Observe a flower garden during the course of a sunny evening; note which colours disappear first, and which remain visible, even gaining in luminosity, as night falls.

Notice the number and types of insects that visit a particular flower, in the course of an afternoon or evening.

Observe the changing patterns of garden fragrance in the course of a day: morning, midday, evening; on warm and cool days; on dry days and immediately after rain.

Make a special effort to combine garden and wild plants in a single display: blackberry, or bramble, and rose; wild grasses and sweet peas; thorn foliage and agapanthus; pinks and burdock; cow parsley or Queen Anne's lace and delphinium; dock and scabious.

Collect old perfume jars, cosmetic jars, even meat-paste jars, for containers and props.

Collect sea shells and coral in quantity, either from their natural source or from craft shops and tropical aquarium shops specializing in marine fish.

Make a cut-foliage display using summer herbs, including variegated as well as plain-leaved types, and perhaps herb flower heads as well.

Collect and carefully observe as many different kinds of wild and garden grass flower heads as possible; use them on their own in a cut-foliage display.

SUMMER TIPS

Gertrude Jekyll, in *Home and Garden*, advises cutting most flowers, with the exception of roses and violets, the day before they are needed, to give them an overnight drink in deep water, since several hours in deep water increases turgidity. Even if this is not possible, cut flowers should never be left lying about, especially in hot sunshine, but placed as soon as they are cut in a bucket with a few inches of water. Picking early in the morning or in the evening is traditionally considered better than picking in the heat of the day, when the water content of flowers and foliage is at its lowest.

Conditioning silver and grey foliage is especially important. The later in the season, and the whiter and more felted or hairy the foliage, the more mature it is, and the longer it is likely to last. Place cut material immediately in a bucket of shallow water. Indoors, hammer the cut end of woody-stemmed material, such as artemisia and *Senecio* 'Sunshine', then give it a long drink. Dip the cut ends of soft material, such as thistle leaves and herbaceous artemisias, in 2.5cm (1in) of boiling water for a few seconds, then give them a long, shallow drink; silver and grey leaves tend to lose their sheen and special quality if soaked.

Delicate, thin leaves, such as hostas early in the season, ferns and the smoke bush (*Cotinus coggygria*) benefit from being sub-merged in water for several hours. An alternative is to dip the cut ends of the foliage into boiling water for 30 seconds, then seal in an airtight polythene bag filled with 45ml (3tbsp) water, for several hours or overnight, before use.

ale salmon-pink gladioli and a few
spikes of white larkspur fill a simple,
two-handled stoneware urn. Re-cutting
gladioli stems every two or three days extends their
cut-flower life, as does removing spent blooms.
Florists often pinch out the top two or three buds, to
encourage the upper florets to open and prevent
curvature of the flower stalk. By leaving the buds
intact, the natural curves of the stem may be used to
add character to a display.

A poppy, delphinium florets, nasturtium, and larkspur create a miniature feast for the eyes. Blue and orange are complementary colours, opposite each other on the colour wheel; juxtaposing them is always exciting. In terms of still-life displays, groups of three tend to be more interesting than pairs or groups of four and asymmetry more interesting than symmetry. Here, two hand-blown antique wine glasses provide the green normally supplied by garden foliage; and an old glass candle jar makes a modest little vase.

cabious, gypsophila, echinops, sweet peas, larkspur and branches of Leycesteria formosa in a seemingly celestial setting. A similar effect can be achieved with boards, or 'flats', wiped with rags dipped in dry poster paint powder or powdered chalk, to create atmospheric backdrops for cut-flower or food displays. Experimenting with a scaled-down flat trains the eye to observe subtle colouring.

• Annuals such as petunias, ageratum and poppies are less liable to wilt if used in a display with their roots intact. Gently wash out as much soil as possible under running water, before placing them in the container. The plant is then lost to the garden, however: a price you may consider too high. Flowers that do wilt can often be revived by re-cutting the stems, then placing them in a deep container of warm water. If Turk's-cap ranunculus or rudbeckia stems go limp, tightly wrap them in newspaper and place them in a bucket of water in a cool spot for several hours. Hydrangeas, violets and roses perk up when completely submerged, flowers and all.

• Frequent re-cutting of agapanthus, rose, antirrhinum, daisy, chrysanthemum, delphinium, foxglove, iris and scabious stems extends their life as cut flowers, and encourages florets to open.

• Large, hollow-stemmed delphiniums and lupins can be up-ended, filled with water, then plugged with cotton wool, to prevent wilting. A 'cottage-garden' aid to prevent lupins wilting is to display them in a dilute instant starch solution. A weak starch solution – 5g (1tsp) per 1l (1½pt) water is also useful for stiffening ferns; submerge them for several hours.

• Carnations, iris and gypsophila are especially vulnerable to

Describing the colour of a rose variety or even a single rose can elude the most competent wordsmith. Roses on the same plant often vary, and colour is rarely uniform even within a flower. Colour may change as the plant matures, and according to its exposure to heat and sunlight. The second, smaller crop of flowers produced in late summer by remontant roses is often a different colour from the first.

ethylene gas, given off by ripe fruit, vegetables and wilting flowers. They and other flowers with fragile petals, such as cosmos, scabious, mallow and violet, also resent draughts, direct sunlight and heat.

• Euphorbia stems contain latex, a milky substance which can block the uptake of water by the stems and foul the vase water. Sear the cut ends, or dip them in boiling water, to prevent wilting. The same treatment suits poppy, hollyhock and phlox.

• Lily pollen can stain hands, clothing and upholstery, as well as the petals, so handle the flowers with care.

• To extend the life of cut stocks, re-cut the stem ends, removing all the lower white portion. Hammer the remaining cut end, or dip it in boiling water, followed by a long drink. Keep the flowers away from direct sunlight, heat and draughts; remove wilted foliage and re-cut the stem ends frequently. Placing a few drops of bleach in the water helps keep it fresh and sweet, as does removing any foliage that would be under water.

• To condition roses, re-cut the stems, dip the cut ends in boiling water for a few seconds, and then give them a drink in a deep bucket or container of water for a couple of hours.

F lorists' large flowered
chrysanthemums absorb some of
the surrounding informality of their
rural setting and their wild daisy 'vase-mates' here.
Almost any flower can be rescued from its florist's
shop connotation, by careful propping, and by
combining with less formal material.

AUTUMN

It was a morning of ground mist, yellow sunshine, and high rifts of blue, white-cloud-dappled sky. The leaves were still thick on the trees, but dew-spangled gossamer threads hung on the bushes and the shrill little cries of unrest of the swallows skimming the green open spaces of the park told of autumn and change.

Lark Rise to Candleford, FLORA THOMPSON, 1876–1947

*F*lorists' chrysan-themums in a setting of autumnal garden foliage lose many of their commercialized overtones. Their poker-straight stems are concealed in the general muddle and rich variety (including the imperfections) of massed leaves and branches, and the overbearing regularity and perfection of the flower heads becomes diluted accordingly.

Just as beauty is always deemed to be in the eye of the beholder, the beginning of autumn is perceived according to a wealth of personal reference points. Astronomers set the first day of autumn, or the autumnal equinox, as 21 September, when the sun crosses the equator and night and day are 12 hours long all over the world. For many children and their parents, however, the first day of autumn is the first day of school. For some, the annual ritual of buying school shoes amid frenzied scenes with unruly toddlers and harassed sales staff grimly marks the end of summer a day or two sooner. For English sportsmen and gourmets, autumn traditionally starts on the 'Glorious Twelfth' of August, when the grouse season opens. And in America, Labour Day Weekend, in early September, with its barbe-cues and trips to the seashore, is followed by the draining of swimming pools and the unspoken acceptance of autumn.

For those who look to nature in general and the garden in particular for signs of seasonal change, the transition from summer to autumn is a gradual one, with cooler and earlier nights and an overblown, blowzy, almost dusty quality in deciduous trees towards the end of August, especially after a dry summer, when one gold-tinged leaf on a dull green sycamore can evoke autumnal thoughts. According to English garden folklore, summer ends when the last foxglove flower falls from the stem, an event that varies from garden to garden. In September, however, parched plants refreshed by rain put on new growth and perhaps flower a second time. Early autumn can seem a second spring, when moderate warmth and humidity create ideal conditions for planting, laying turf and sowing seed.

*A*n unlikely setting in reality, this is nonetheless a pleasing collection of autumnal treasures: apples in an old terracotta tub, and garden foliage in an old garden urn. Cotoneaster, complete with berries, photinia and maple almost overflow their container, capturing the spirit of abundance that is so much a part of autumn.

For those who garden and enjoy displaying garden flowers and foliage in the home, autumn is less related to the fixed points of the calendar, much as some people would like it to be, than to random weather patterns. Delightfully warm Indian summers, autumnal gales and the first hard frosts determine whether the autumnal leaf colours last for weeks, days or hours; and whether there will be the lovely option of displaying late-blooming roses with winter-flowering jasmine. Immediately before the first frost, whenever it occurs, the last roses and dahlias should be picked, complete with the unopened buds that were left untouched during the growing season, and which make naturally beautiful companions to the open blooms. It is also the moment for picking masses of annuals, or bringing pots of flowering annuals and tender perennials indoors for a final, glorious display.

In spite of the abundance often found in autumn gardens and the warmth of autumnal colours, the autumnal mood can be bleak, with its symbolic undertones of incipient decay. Summer holidays and vacations are over, cooler temperatures and early evenings are setting in and the spectre of the first frost looms, with the death of annuals. The Victorians, great ones for emotional self-indulgence, blamed or even nurtured many a despair on autumn. In fact, nature only mirrors internal moods, and autumn in the garden presents much that is positive, for those in a frame of mind to observe it. Spring's hazel catkin buds, for example, are fully formed and visible in autumn before the leaves even fall. The robin returns to autumnal gardens, after a summer's absence, as noted in an old poem from *The Christian Year*:

> To the Redbreast
> Unheard in summer's flaring ray,
> Pour forth thy notes, sweet singer,
> Wooing the stillness of the autumn day;
> Bid it a moment linger,
> Nor fly
> Too soon from winter's scowling eye.

Autumnal leaf fall is in itself a positive act, preparing plants for a vital period of rest, preventing possible snow damage by removing most of the surface mass and returning organic nutrients and bulk to the soil. Even in cities, autumn can be uplifting, especially those noted for their park land, and is considered by many to be the most beautiful season in London and New York.

Light often affects mood, and though early autumnal evenings can be depressing, early October mornings can be magical, with grey mists creating a backdrop against which flower colours glow. Lengthening autumnal shadows add depth to the changing landscape and, on a smaller scale, to indoor flower displays, making them more interesting than in the flat light of high summer. And there is a singularly attractive yellow light on sunny autumn afternoons, of a penetrating clarity.

*P*umpkins, apples, pot marigolds, the
fruits and foliage of the guelder rose
(*Viburnum opulus*) and rosehips provide a
typical autumnal riot of colour, here made even
more riotous by the backdrop of brightly patterned
fabric. This combination of fruits, foliage, flowers
and fabric is a good example of the total integration
of a setting and the objects within it – an approach
more akin to painting than flower arranging.

*D*omestic objects can become *objets d'art* meriting close observation when used to 'prop' an arrangement (right). Here, an old-fashioned cake mould and salad drainers combine with ripe Chinese lanterns and weather-blackened cow parsley seed heads.

*O*range gladioli against a blue background (below) forego subtlety in favour of direct and powerful colour contrast, much used in Art Deco. Autumnal variations on the theme of orange and blue are potentially endless; blue Michaelmas daisies, late aconites and hydrangeas; and orange dahlias, marigolds, even roses.

AUTUMN COLOURS

Autumnal colours are mostly warm ones, ranging from the rich yellows of chrysanthemums and dahlias, old golds of achilleas and oranges of Chinese lanterns to the reds, wines and purples of dying vine foliage and the warm mauves of Michaelmas daisies. Orange, probably the most typical autumn colour, is midway on the spectrum between yellow and red, but under the general umbrella of its name includes various proportions of each, from rich, buttery yellow-orange to flaming scarlet. Clear orange is the core colour of calendulas, or pot marigolds, nasturtiums and African marigolds, high summer annuals that flower boldly until the first autumn frosts.

It is also the broad colour range of montbretias, curtonus, red-hot pokers, tiger lilies, gaillardias and rudbeckias, flowers at their prime in late summer, continuing into September. In terms of foliage, many of the Japanese maples and flowering cherries turn orange, as do the smoke bush (*Cotinus coggygria*), spindles, deciduous cotoneasters and azaleas. The berries and fruits of cotoneaster, pyracantha and crab apples can also be orange and scarlet.

Orange is a hard colour to live with on a large scale, but abundantly available now and richly rewarding if used well. It was a popular colour in the twenties, especially in the Art Deco period. (This severe decorative style was influenced by the then fashionable

93

Cubism, Egyptology, Diaghilev's 'Ballet Russe' and contemporary French furniture as exhibited in the 1925 'Exposition Internationale des Arts Décoratifs et Industriels Modernes', whence Art Deco got its name.) Orange and blue, complementaries on the colour wheel, feature heavily in the ceramics of Clarice Cliff, and orange enjoyed a brief comeback in the fifties.

Nowadays, interior designers shy away from clear orange, and bright orange clothing usually ends up prominently marked down at end-of-season sales. Perhaps this is because orange is a particularly flat colour in large doses, such as on painted walls, and particularly unkind to pale skin, draining it of visual warmth. It may also be because the high yellow content in orange makes it a bright, vibrant hue, attracting, holding and then tiring the eye. Lastly, so many airport lounges and fast-food restaurants feature orange upholstery and orange plastic seats and table tops, that it has become the modern-day colour of transit rather than repose.

Fortunately, no flower, leaf or berry colour is completely flat in tone. The shadows within the petals of an orange cactus dahlia or chrysanthemum, the gradations from orange to scarlet on a snowy mespilus leaf, and the browny-black calyx and stalk on the end of an orange rosehip, all help to 'tame' the colour. Since fresh flowers, by their nature, are short-lived, spending five days in the presence of a brilliant orange dahlia is less of a commitment than spending two years with a brilliant orange winter coat, or ten years with a vibrant orange living room. Then, too, a display of flowers in the home (as opposed to a vast bedding-out scheme in a public park) is rarely large enough for any colour, even orange, to be overwhelming, and a tiny amount of orange in a multicoloured display can act like a flash of light, enlivening far beyond its relative size.

Colour combinations containing orange that sound dreadful can look wonderful, depending on proportions, lighting, setting and form. Despite what books that set out 'approved' lists of colour combinations might say, there really are no hard and fast rules on the subject. Orange seen against the pink, blue and mauve range of Michaelmas daisies, for example, is often stunningly successful. Choosing between almost identical shades of russet in different chrysanthemum varieties might seem pointless, though one russet shade may look brilliant with orange calendulas and another

*T*hose who find Chinese lanterns boring material for floral displays should look again. The unripe lantern-shaped calyces are brilliant green, while those in transition range from pale green to pale yellow and old gold. Try using green calyces in fresh-flower displays, and drying green and transitional as well as orange calyces. If you leave some unpicked, at the end of winter you may find attractive skeletonized lanterns, with only lace-like traceries of veins left.

disastrous. Then, too, fashions change, and the pinks, oranges and lime-greens of the Sixties for example, will undoubtedly reassert themselves at some future time. When dealing with orange or any other 'difficult' colour, experiment with various combinations, and try them in different proportions, using your eyes, not preconceived notions, as a reference point.

Unless you are aiming for the anonymous 'hotel-lobby' style of flower display, colour combinations are meant to be expressive, in the same way that speaking is. As, depending on mood and circumstances, sometimes whispering is appropriate, so at other times is shouting. Therefore while flowers have inherent connotations of peacefulness, you may want to express exuberance or unbridled exhilaration through colour, especially in a neutral setting that invites a bright floral statement and focal point. Autumn provides an infinite range of exuberant combinations, some self-contained within a single plant. The communal garden fishbone cotoneaster (C. horizontalis), for example, is studded with round scarlet-orange berries set against its own crimson leaves. Cultivars of rowan combine brilliant autumn leaf colour with equally brilliant berries: the deep-pink berries and orange and red leaves of *Sorbus vilmorinii*; and the red, orange and purple leaves of *Sorbus* 'Joseph Rock', with its bright yellow berries. The rugosa roses, especially the white-flowered 'Blanc Double de Coubert' and the wine-red-flowered 'Roseraie de l'Hay' combine yellow autumn foliage and attractive, bright-red hips.

Orange and blue, being complementaries, intensify each other when seen together, and this is true not only for the human eye. Nature combines orange or yellow-orange with blue or blue-violet in many single flowers such as lupins, pansies, buddleias and forget-me-nots, because this contrast is instantly attractive to bees, guiding them to pollen and nectar, thus aiding pollination. In the case of the orange sepals and blue petals of the bird of paradise flower (*Strelitzia reginae*), the combination is particularly inviting to its bird pollinators.

For experiments with orange and blue at this time of year, there are autumnal gentians, aconites, tradescantias, late cornflowers, *Ceanothus* 'Autumnal Blue' and even the odd delphinium to oblige. (Gertrude Jekyll, the great English turn-of-the-century garden designer, suggested planting orange lilies and blue delphiniums in close proximity, so that each could enhance the brilliance of the other.) By the beginning of autumn, hydrangeas are turning from clear blue to a more subtle, overcast hue, but they are lovely for contrasting with montbretias, nasturtiums and even the glowing orange of some roses, such as the coppery orange 'Just Joey', 'Orangeade' or 'Orange Sensation'. The most intense autumnal blue of all comes from the little hardy plumbago (*Ceratostigma willmottianum*), whose own autumnal leaves of crimson, gold and green make a perfect setting for its blooms, and those of other species.

Orange can also be 'cooled' with silver foliage such as that of *Senecio* 'Sunshine', garden sage or artichoke leaves, or made to glow

ellow, orange, pink, scarlet, purple and
maroon is a colour combination liable to
rejection when described in words, but
magical when seen. Flowers, foliage and berries set
in a collection of lustreware jugs capture the gradual
transition from summer to autumn. From the left,
Venetian smoke bush and maple leaves; sorbus
berries; salvia; anemones; and mallow, antirrhinum,
flowering tobacco and Michaelmas daisies.

97

against a background of dark-green or brown foliage, for example, glycerined beech or chestnut foliage, or glossy camellia leaves. Orange and wine-red can be riveting, especially if one or both hues appears in gradations. Orange with a bevy of hot colours can express the glory of gardening and *joie de vivre* combined (see the illustration on pages 100–1).

Nature provides many options to explore in autumn: orange muted with other hues or tinged with white becomes the evocatively named apricot, peach, tangerine and salmon shades. Chrysanthemums, particularly, come in warm colours of an almost infinite range; looking at a chrysanthemum specialist's illustrated catalogue is like looking at an artist's palette, where every possible tone, tint and shade of orange is explored in little dabs and strokes.

AUTUMN LEAVES

Because the backdrop of autumn leaves is such a large proportion of the rural and suburban landscape, and because urban trees form the main link with natural seasonal cycles in cities, foliage colour influences our perception of this season in particular. Autumn leaves are freely available, from public parks as well as private gardens, and the possibilities of making decorative use of them indoors are so easy and obvious that they are often overlooked.

Leaves turn colour in autumn because the dropping temperatures and light levels cause decreased root activity, which in turn means that less sap reaches the leaves. Chlorophyll, which gives a leaf its green colour, breaks down in autumn, and carotenoid pigments build up in some leaves, turning them pale yellow. Other pigments also replace the chlorophyll: anthocyanin produces purple, red, crimson and scarlet leaf colouring; and anthoxanthin produces golden yellow.

The best autumn leaf colours occur on acid soil, and where hot summers are followed by sharp night frosts, as for example in the North American New England states. The same species not only vary in their autumnal show from year to year, but from one location to another – often a cause for disappointment when the tree or shrub in one's garden fails to live up to expectations as built up by illustrated gardening books and catalogues. Many woody and herbaceous plants produce the best autumn leaf colour if 'starved' on poor, dry soil: the smoke bush (*Cotinus coggygria*), stag's horn sumach and sedums, for example.

Leaves in full autumn colour can be used as cut material, but they are short-lived, and never sold commercially for this reason. By the time leaves have turned colour, the point where the leaf stalk meets the stem has hardened, forming a hollow 'separating layer'. This layer protects the stem during winter, but gradually detaches the leaf, making it vulnerable to the first gust of wind and unable to take up moisture, whether sap or water in a vase. If you have a garden full of autumn foliage, or even a single Virginia creeper, then replacing drooping foliage with fresh every day is no problem.

Red, orange, yellow and purple autumnal foliage has instant

The flaming, vibrant colours of autumnal foliage embody the visual richness of the season. Here, leaves of Japanese maple, flowering cherry, crab apple and *Parrotia persica* are displayed at the height of their beauty. A wide, shallow bowl filled with autumn foliage, placed on a dining-room table or coffee table, encourages close observation of individual leaves, in comfort and at leisure. Cool temperatures and a fine mist spray of water add extra life to this naturally short-lived display.

99

A study of autumnal yellows, oranges and reds. From left to right, back row, are *Mahonia japonica* foliage, nasturtium and feverfew, and pot marigolds. From left to right, front row, are nasturtium, poppy, rose and winter-flowering jasmine. Looking closely at a garden in autumn makes nonsense of rigidly compartmentalizing plants into separate seasons. Here, for example, roses and winter-flowering jasmine overlap quite naturally. Winter-flowering viburnum can also be had in early autumn, and *Prunus subhirtella* 'Autumnalis' flowers in winter and spring as well as autumn.

appeal, but brown autumnal foliage is often overlooked and under-used. Among many traditional flower arrangers, brown is literally a 'dirty' word, a colour that doesn't appear in the spectrum and therefore somehow doesn't count. The new breed of professional advisors who set out how to succeed in the business world, including how to 'dress for success', inform us with total assurance that 'brown is down', the colour of failure as presumably opposed to black and navy blue. But brown is also the colour of nature and natural products: of bark and wood, of leather, nuts and semi-precious stones such as amber and onyx, of hair, skin and animal fur, and of ploughed fields, Harris tweeds and many autumn leaves.

Brown does not instantly attract and hold the eye, but if everything attracted the eye in equal measure, the eye would tire quickly. (There are few brown flowers, with the notable exception of carrion flowers, whose colour and odour resemble rotting flesh –

irresistible to pollinating blowflies, but hardly good material for cut-flower displays.)

Browns are made up of two or more colours: orange and blue, red and green, and purple and yellow make brown when mixed together. As any child with a paint box knows, the more different colours are mixed together, the 'muddier', or browner, they become. Muddy may have negative connotations, and muted is perhaps a better word. A great unifier, a mass of brown leaves can make strident floral colour combinations seem comfortable together.

Brown air-dried (see page 122) beech, oak and field maple leaves often remain on the tree well into autumn and even into winter. (With oak, it is usually the lowest branches, handy for reaching with secateurs.) Bracken air-dries naturally, in shades from pale beige to russet. Hosta's decorative leaves and the pleated, sword-like leaves of *Curtonus paniculatus* will also air-dry successfully.

An old oil painting of a rural scene sets the tone for this autumnal display, based on yellows and browns. From left to right are the bauble-like dried seed heads of *Filipendula*, flat yellow achillea flower heads, greater and lesser quaking grass, fresh cow parsley and Russet apples. Some apple varieties, such as Russet and Cox's Orange Pippin, have subtle variations in skin texture and tone which make them more interesting, perhaps even more 'believable' as fruits of the earth, than perfectly flat-toned, highly polished and identically shaped varieties, such as Granny Smith.

*T*erracotta flower pots filled with apples, and an old tin jug with pelargoniums and sprigs of variegated ivy, set against vine leaves in full autumnal colour, present not so much a flower arrangement as an evocative still life. Stuffing a deep container with crumpled newspaper, then finishing with a thick layer of fruit would create the same feeling of abundance with less than abundant props. It would also work with other ornamental objects: water-washed pebbles, for example, or potpourri.

All are ideal for combining with late autumn flowers, especially for giving rather uniform florists' chrysanthemums a home-grown appeal they normally lack. When using air-dried foliage with fresh flowers, try to rest or balance the stems above the water level in the container, otherwise the leaves are liable to rot.

Glycerined foliage (see page 122) provides even richer browns, and lasts indefinitely, in both fresh and dried flower displays. (If used in water, dry thoroughly before storing between uses.) The process also retains foliage flexibility, making glycerined leaves more lifelike and less vulnerable than brittle, bone-dry ones. As well as recreating autumnal tones of deciduous foliage, such as beech, glycerine can also give rich autumnal tints to evergreen foliage such as camellia, that normally remains green all year round. Trees whose leaves are suitable for glycerining include maple, birch, sweet chestnut, chamaecyparis, cypress, eucalyptus, laurel, bay, oak and rowan. Suitable shrubs include evergreen berberis, box, camellia, Mexican orange, fishbone cotoneaster (*C. horizontalis*), heather, eleagnus, butcher's broom, escallonia, evergreen magnolia and viburnum. Even spotted laurel, so difficult to use in its natural state, loses its spots when glycerined and becomes a deep browny black. You can also glycerine herbaceous foliage such as bergenia, evergreen helle-bore, lady's mantle, hosta and paeony leaves.

AUTUMN CONTAINERS

Because autumn is associated with harvesting and storing food, kitchen and garden implements seem particularly apt containers at

alus, or ornamental crab apples, are displayed simply and unpretentiously in a lustreware jug set against an Oriental cotton printed fabric. Imperfection is part of nature, especially in autumn, as flowers, fruit and foliage show the effects of several months' weather and perhaps disease or insect attack. Including slightly flawed material (as opposed to totally ruined!) adds interest and uniqueness, and helps capture the essence of this season.

this time. And because autumn is also associated with maturity, old, even battered, containers are especially suitable. Wicker baskets and woven wooden trugs, ceramic and wooden bowls, jugs, pitchers and teapots, storage jars, old decorative tins, tin mugs and pots all have potential.

Ceramic, terracotta, porcelain and enamelled tin containers with a cracked, chipped or broken glaze often end up on the bric-a-brac stalls of fêtes, jumble sales and charity bazaars. From the forties and fifties come hand-painted vases and jugs of a soft, plaster-like material which, once chipped, has the quality of much painted and weathered stonework, rather like that of old Mediterranean buildings. All are worth collecting; the surface patterns of crazes, underglaze and even rust can add seasoned character to a floral display.

Globe artichoke heads have been allowed to go to seed purely for reasons of beauty. As well as thistles in their prime, an overblown, blackened thistle head is included, perhaps as a floral allegory of the nature of autumn. The ornamental cabbage is a relatively new addition to the house-plant scene, and remains attractive for weeks in a cool room, or for months in a window box.

Obviously, there is a fine dividing line between tastefully weathered and 'distressed' containers, and those that simply appear broken and dreary, unworthy even of jumble sales. That dividing line, like the dividing line between summer and autumn itself, is in the eye of the beholder.

Metallic containers, especially simple copper and brass ones, have a warm reflective quality, empathetic to the warm autumnal palette, while pewter has a muted appeal. Lustreware (pottery given a shiny metallic coating emulating silver, copper, gold or platinum, and fired in a special process to prevent oxidizing) is lovely filled with autumnal leaves, flowers and foliage. Popular in Victorian times, lustreware is now something of a collector's item, and worth investing in. There are many attractive styles which combine metallic glaze with solid colours and decorative, transfer-printed or hand-painted patterns.

It is interesting how tastes change. The Victorians used highly decorative ceramic cachepots to hide the terracotta flower pots in which their houseplants grew. Today, terracotta flower pots can themselves be decorative objects, and if faded by weather or encrusted with moss and lichen, so much the better. And many humble Victorian kitchen implements that never left the kitchen, such as jelly-moulds and jugs, today take pride of place in collections of containers for displaying flowers and foliage.

AUTUMN EXTRAS

Props and backdrops are not only the prerogative of photographers, although they, and the graphic designers who crop their pictures, have rather more artistic leeway than the normal householder. Nonetheless, everyday objects can be arranged to reinforce the colours or mood of an autumn floral display, while the objects themselves often take on newly rediscovered beauty.

Richly coloured fabrics – old paisley shawls and silk scarves, for example, can be presented as smooth, mini-tablecloths, wrapped round the base of the container, or round the rim, neckerchief style. For more drama, fabric can be fixed to extend vertically behind the display, as well as beneath it.

In the case of kitchen and garden-derived containers, implements or similar containers can be clustered nearby; a mixture of empty and flower-filled jugs; a mixture of flower-filled jelly moulds and empty, even upturned ones; and tiny glass jars containing a single 'afterthought' flower or leaf, for closer observation.

Fruit and vegetables are traditional autumnal objects, so much so that they are often unjustly dismissed as boring. Rediscovering the beauty of fruit and vegetables is a standard project for art students. Try doing some pencil drawings of quartered cauliflowers, halved green peppers or even mounds of pulses, to study natural form and shadow in minute detail.

Thanks to modern agriculture and transport, most fruits and vegetables are available most, if not all, of the year, but some crops still have particularly autumnal overtones: apples, quinces,

A single pelargonium floret, figs, grapes, pomegranates, plums, *Sedum sieboldii* 'Medio-variegatum', *Ceropegia woodii*, and a cactus on an old wooden tray. The cool purple backdrop is reminiscent of Shelley's verse:

'Tis the noon of autumn glow
When a soft and purple mist
Like a vaporous amethyst . .
fills the overflowing sky.

pomegranates, gourds, nuts, Indian corn, grain and root vegetables. As autumn progresses, the proportion of flowers and foliage to edible produce can easily be reversed, and just a few flowers can 'prop' a display of fruits and vegetables (see the illustration on pages 116–17). Ripening fruit and vegetables release ethylene gas which can adversely affect flowers, causing them to wilt and die prematurely. Obviously, dried flowers and fruit or vegetables can be combined with impunity; fortunately, chrysanthemums, dahlias and most other autumnal flowers are fairly tolerant.

Game is an autumnal food, and though often depicted in old still lifes, most people find dead game birds in close proximity off-putting. Still, pheasant feathers can usually be bought (with or without the pheasant) from country butchers. A glass full of handsomely coloured tail feathers (pop them in the microwave for a couple of minutes, if freshly plucked and still moist, to sterilize them) acts as a vertical emphasis, or combine them with dried materials for a long-lasting display. Alternatively, send away for catalogues from fishing-tackle suppliers specializing in fly-tying; feathers, on and off the wing and breast, are available from native and exotic birds.

This floral vignette has painted and printed flowers covering every possible surface. From left to right are a bunch of helipterum; an old hand-painted tea pot with larkspur seed pods; a Victorian jug with dried gypsophila and a single paper rose; a blue-and-white tea pot with sea lavender; a hand-painted jug with hydrangea and gypsophila; a shallow dish of helichrysum flower heads; and an honesty-filled jug.

AUTUMN SETTINGS

The great rural outdoors is the most congenial backdrop for a mass of autumn flowers, and if you're entertaining in your garden, it's an opportunity to present a mass of fresh-cut flowers and foliage in a sympathetic setting. Otherwise, a windowsill overlooking an attractive garden scene is the next best thing. In south- and west-facing windows, the direct, low light has the effect of darkening the flowers by comparison, in the same way that taking holiday snaps facing into the sun makes the people photographed come out as silhouettes. On the other hand, some flowers such as sweet peas, and foliage such as the smoke bush (*Cotinus coggygria*), are exquisitely translucent, and direct light through them creates an unworldly beauty.

Most studio photographers will have access to a selection of large wooden surfaces for backdrops: polished mahogany, stripped pine, weathered oak (perhaps the odd barn door) and old wooden doors with layers and layers of chipped paint. The idea of keeping such a supply in an ordinary home is unrealistic, but a small panel of old wood can serve as a setting for flowers, especially if the alternative is busy or mundane wallpaper. Paintings, posters or coloured prints of country scenes make good backdrops for autumn displays, or even large illustrated art books open to a suitable page. Harvesting is the most primordial, and perhaps the most positive, activity associated with this time of year, and harvest prints and paintings are especially apt. Many Persian rugs have rich autumnal tones, especially those made with natural dyes and faded with use and time. Small rugs can be used as tablecloths or wall hangings.

AUTUMN INSPIRATIONS, OBSERVATIONS AND PROJECTS

• The countryside and large urban open spaces, such as London's Richmond Park and New York's Central Park, offer endless ideas for combinations of colours and forms. Inspiration can come from the random, momentary patterns made by a pile of wind-blown leaves or a flock of ducks bobbing about in the water, or from the more deliberate juxtaposition of plants in a shrubbery.

• Rather than simply absorbing the general radiance or mood of an afternoon, with details melting one into another and soon forgotten, take photographs to help focus the mind on particularly strong combinations and compositions. Film and processing are so cheap and cameras so simple to operate, that photography is the modern equivalent to a sketchbook or notepad.

• Photographing the same tree every two or three days, as it turns from summer to autumnal colours and finally to its leafless winter state, is a way of studying changing colour proportions, and their effect on how an individual colour is seen. A small area of yellow or orange, for example, seen against a large area of green, seems much more vivid and bright than that same hue with the proportions reversed.

• Collect, over as long a time span as the weather allows, masses of bright and subtly coloured autumn leaves. Make sure they are dry, then press them between the pages of telephone directories for at

*H*ybrid tea roses flower well on into autumn, given reasonable weather. Here, 'Precious Platinum' is displayed in a blue glass vase against an old pitted mirror, giving a lovely background texture. 'Precious Platinum' is heavily fragrant and rain resistant, but prone to mildew; fortunately, there are now easy-to-apply, multi-purpose rose sprays, combining nutrients with fungicides.

*S*hown here are end-of-season poppies with clusters of *Sorbus* berries, lustreware jugs and an upturned Victorian copper jelly mould. *Papaver somniferum* buds and unripe seed pods are included, because both are beautiful in their own way and contribute a sense of time passing to the display.

least two weeks, or iron them between sheets of waxed paper with the iron set to cool. Glue the leaves to card to make a collage, going from cool to warm colours as a controlled exercise in visual perception, or just create a pretty pattern. Display bowls of newly gathered brightly coloured leaves, just as they are, or thoroughly washed and tucked in amongst fruit, gourds or nuts. The effect may last only a day, but it is long enough to grace the dining table of a dinner party or family meal.

Collect ornamental and wild foliage, flowers, grasses and seed heads for drying (see page 122). Although country hedgerows and woodlands are more fertile hunting grounds than cities, even empty building sites, car parks and the front gardens of vacant houses can usually provide dock, thistle, buddleia, ground elder and rose-bay willow herb seed heads at the very least, and often more. These are obviously prolific survivors, but do make sure nothing you pick is a protected species, and if in doubt leave well alone. Local libraries can provide lists of protected species, which vary from country to

As well as the fiery colours of flame, autumn foliage can resemble the soft and sombre tones of smoke. Such autumnal leaf colours are often a feature of alkaline, as opposed to acid, soils. Here, maple, horse chestnut, sorbus, tulip tree, flowering cherry, and plane form a subtle collage, studded with occasional hydrangea florets, in their own smoky-blue autumnal tones.

country. Unless you have a large garden and a great deal of time, concentrate on material not commercially grown, since virtually all the everlastings, or immortelles, plus annual and perennial statice, are cheap and readily available from florists. Garden-flower seed pods worth drying include acanthus, agapanthus, columbine, pot marigold, tall-growing bellflowers, larkspur, foxglove, iris, St John's wort, lychnis, leopard's bane, cranesbill, montbretia, alstroemeria, grape hyacinth, evening primrose, paeony, rudbeckia, echinops and paper moon scabious. With all these plants, you get the full enjoyment of the flowers first. Garden flowers worth drying include astilbe, cornflower, hop, sedum, mallow, chives, allium, sweet William, heather, mint, hydrangeas and rosebuds.

• Collect foliage for glycerining (see page 104). Ivy, rose and *Sorbus* berries, too, can be preserved in glycerine, though most remain plump for two weeks or more in their natural state.

• Visit an open-air fruit and vegetable market. Observe and sketch or photograph the piles of fruits and vegetables for sale.

An unexpected but beautiful combination of silvery grey pewter, grey satin brocade with its own yellowed lining, and ripe figs, plums, turnips and blueberries. Their different textures affect how the light reflects off each one, and add rich subtlety to the display. Yellow heads of craspedia, a member of the *Compositae* family grown for drying, introduce a brighter note.

Record and colour combinations. Buy the most attractive fruits and vegetables, even in small quantities, and try to recreate their open-air, unpretentious beauty indoors. Buy gourds for drying.

• Observe autumnal game: the breast, wing and tail feathers of a brace of pheasants, for example, noting the subtler colouring of the female. The skin of freshly caught brown trout has equally beautiful surface patterns of black and orange dots and silver glints.

• Much decorative art is based on nature, often deriving its pigments as well as its forms from natural sources. Observe, for example, the colours and patterns of old Turkish and Oriental carpets. Collecting them is beyond the means of most people, but major auction houses have regular carpet sales, and viewing days are open to the public. Primitive and primitive-style pottery is often decorated with rich earth colours, ideal as a starting point for an autumnal colour scheme.

• Collect fabrics – ends of lines, end-of-season sales, oddments – in rich autumnal tones and floral patterns. Fringe or hem the edges, and use as reference for possible colour combinations, or for propping displays, either as a backdrop or tablecloth. Paisley scarves and shawls make instant props; second-hand ones are cheaper and often more characterful than new ones.

• With open eyes and an open mind, inspiration can even come from refuse. Observe the contents of skips, especially on building sites; old painted doors and window frames often have pleasing textures and patterns within the flaking paint, and old mirrors, such as the one shown on page 113, can have intriguing and subtle patterning. Buildings in the process of demolition often reveal elevations that are themselves like abstract works of art: the colours of walls, one room against another, joined and bisected by the diagonals of halls and stairs.

• Lastly, observe, and be prepared to raid, bonfire heaps; attractive branches, complete with air-dried leaves, can often be extracted.

AUTUMN TIPS

• Chrysanthemum and Michaelmas daisies, archetypal autumnal flowers, last longer if their stems are cut, dipped briefly in boiling water, then given a long, cool drink before being placed in a display. The stems easily become blocked, so they should be re-cut occasionally during the course of the display. The tiny flowers of the

Gourds lie in the open, after a hard frost, providing the last defiant colour in the garden before submitting to the winter. Edible and ornamental gourds are so much a part of autumn that their decorative potential is often overlooked. Display a bowl of gourds nestling in autumn leaves, either fresh or dried; or with nuts, pebbles or potpourri.

Michaelmas daisy and the larger 'daisies' of spray chrysanthemums open, flower and die over ten days or more. Using nail scissors or thumb and forefinger, pinch off the first of the dead flowers, as they are unattractive and prevent later buds opening.

In country markets, flower stalls sometimes sell 'seconds' of fresh, commercially grown chrysanthemums. These may have shorter- or thinner-than-normal stems, which curve rather than remain rigidly upright; fewer flowers per spray, in the case of spray 'mums'; or smaller flowers, in the case of huge incurved, intermediate or reflexed varieties. Not only are these 'seconds' excellent value for money, but they tend to have a garden-like grace missing from the 'first-quality' types, with their look of machined perfection and unnatural size.

Small pompon dahlias are usually longer-lasting as cut flowers than the larger types. Treat dahlia stems as for chrysanthemums and Michaelmas daisies; an old-fashioned way of conditioning large, hollow-stemmed dahlias is to up-end them, fill the stems with water, and plug them with a wad of cotton wool.

The foliage of chrysanthemums, Michaelmas daisies, dahlias and autumnal annuals such as China asters and pot marigolds is traditionally removed before the flowers are used in a display. This is for several reasons. The foliage below the surface of the water quickly rots, encouraging the growth of bacteria, which causes the stems to rot in their turn and the flowers to die prematurely. Foliage also diverts water from the flower heads, shortening the life of the display. In addition, many people find the foliage dull. Though it is sensible to remove foliage below the water line, whether other foliage is removed is a personal choice, and leaving it intact looks more natural. Least successful, visually, is to remove a long-stemmed flower's own foliage, and display the 'naked' stem, unrelieved by other foliage or flowers.

Anemone stems are naturally leafless and graceful, but are heavy drinkers, and their containers may need frequent topping up. (Anemones do not last at all well when inserted in florists' foam!) The stems also tend to lean towards a directional source of light, such as a window. Either turn the container round regularly, or accept this wilfulness as part of nature.

Zinnias are long-lasting as cut flowers, but the stems sometimes droop from the weight of the large flower heads. Inserting a wire or fine stick up the centre of the stem is a traditional solution, but it looks more natural if the stem is shortened and the flower tucked into the base of a display. If zinnia stems are wilted and floppy, from being out of water for some time, re-cut the stem ends, then wrap the flowers tightly in newspaper and place them up to their heads in cold water overnight.

Montbretia and curtonus flowers are particularly vulnerable to ethylene gas, so keep them away from ripening fruit and vegetables and dying flowers. Remove their own lower flowers as they shrivel, for the sake of appearance and to encourage the upper buds to open.

To intensify the colour of autumn foliage without giving it a

*H*and-thrown terracotta pots of dried flowers fill a windowsill with autumnal colour. From the left are deep-purple winged statice, hydrangea, Russian or rat's-tail statice, pale-lavender winged statice, and *Limonium suworowii*, a species of sea lavender. Flowers resting horizontally, as if about to be arranged, add a note of informality. Though fresh flowers can be photographed in this state, it is not a long-term option. Dried flowers, however, can be in a perpetual state of rest with a pleasing end result.

gloss, paint it lightly with polyurethane varnish. This also gives nuts and gourds a richer, deeper colour.

To get the maximum life from woody-stemmed material, such as guelder rose (*Viburnum opulus*), sorbus, viburnum and mahonia, hammer the lowest 2.5cm (1in) of stem, then give them a long, deep drink. The cut woody ends of ornamental vine foliage, such as that shown on page 104, should be singed or dipped briefly in boiling water, before being given a long drink in 15cm (6in) of water.

DRYING AND PRESERVING

Always pick material for drying on a dry day, as surface and trapped moisture rots the material before it can dry. To dry hydrangea heads, pick them when the petal-like bracts start to feel papery. They dry perfectly well hung upside down in a well-ventilated spot out of direct sunlight, but they can also be 'water dried', by placing the cut stems in a small tumbler of water. As the water is absorbed and evaporates, the hydrangea head dries. Hosta leaves can also be dried in this way.

To dry rosebuds, simply hang them upside down in a warm, dry, airy spot. Make sure that they are fully dried before removing them, otherwise they are liable to bend at the neck.

To dry gourds, choose those with at least a short stump of stem intact. Wipe any surface dirt away, then pat dry. Make a tiny pinprick through the skin, then place on a mesh screen or rack in a warm, dry, well-ventilated spot such as an airing cupboard. Turn them over occasionally; when they feel very light in relation to their size, and make a hollow sound when rapped with the knuckles, they are dry and only then should they be varnished.

To dry ornamental grasses and grains, pick them when unripe and green, or not quite fully ripe and golden. (Most material continues ripening when drying, and if picked fully ripe is liable to become overripe and shatter.) Hang them upside down in bunches, or, in the case of grasses, dry the right way up for a natural-looking curved stem.

To glycerine foliage, pick branches of fully mature leaves before they begin to take on autumnal tints in late summer or early autumn and as soon as possible before glycerining. Crush the lowest 2.5cm (1in) of stem and place in a tall, narrow container filled with a half-and-half mixture of thoroughly stirred glycerine and hot water. When the uppermost leaves feel leathery, the process is complete: this may take anything from under a week in the case of small, thin leaves such as fishbone cotoneaster, to nearly two months in the case of evergreen magnolia.

*D*ried okra, annual and perennial sea lavender, Chinese lanterns, hydrangeas, helichrysums, love-in-a-mist, poppies and helipterums are all used here to form a large-scale room decoration hung from a trellis panel.

*H*ellebores in variety, snowdrops,
hardy cyclamen leaves and sprigs of
lavender foliage are freshly gathered and
tightly bunched. Hellebores are notoriously tricky as
cut flowers: pricking the stems in several places
releases trapped air, as does drawing a pin from just
under the flower to the bottom of the cut stem.

124

WINTER

Throughout January, and indeed from the middle of December, is the time when outdoor flowers for cutting and for house decoration are most scarce; and yet there are Christmas Roses and yellow Jasmine and Laurustinus.... A very few flowers can be made to look well if cleverly arranged with plenty of good foliage; and even when a hard and long frost spoils the few blooms that would otherwise be available, leafy branches alone are beautiful in rooms.

'*Wood and Garden*', GERTRUDE JEKYLL, 1843–1932

It is interesting, and indicative of how divorced from the reality of the seasons modern life can be, that fashionable winter clothing is first shown by designers and shops in the height of summer. The frozen food industry has ensured that virtually all fruits and vegetables are available in winter, however brief and distant their natural season; and commercial growers for the floristry industry can induce the least likely flowers to bloom in winter, lily of the valley, lilac and quelder rose (*Viburnum opulus*) among them. Nevertheless, many people still enjoy making direct contact with the seasons, and cut-flower and foliage displays are one way to do it.

Technically, the winter solstice occurs on 20 December, close enough to Christmas for the two to merge in many children's minds. (25 December was probably set arbitrarily by the Church to coincide with existing pagan festivities marking the winter solstice; early proponents of Christianity tried to overlay pagan festivals and sites with Christian significance, rather than to abolish them.) And if Christmas does not mark the start of winter for children, then Christmas holidays from school do.

To those who garden, the first hard frost usually means the arrival of winter, even if it occurs in late October. Frost kills the last lingering annuals, but also brings out the beauty of willows, dog-woods, birches, alders and cherries with coloured bark. Frost enhances the extraordinary white stems of the ornamental bramble, *Rubus cockburnianus*; and the stalwart ever-grey *Senecio* 'Sun-shine'. Hoar frost, frozen water vapour deposited in clear, still weather, transforms weeds and dead stems into frozen lace and web-like finery, and lawns become a fragile crystal carpet. The transform-ation is only temporary, of course, and in the sun's warmth weeds and stems revert to a soggier version of their ordinary selves.

Darkness comes soon after tea in Great Britain, with its more northerly latitude than America, and restricts gardening to a few short hours each day. Winter light is low and weak, but it can also throw dramatically long shadows. Thin wintry mists act like gauze over a camera lens in early morning, softening and removing the mundane quality from even the most familiar view.

Winter, like any other season, is unpredictable in its weather pattern. Great pleasure can be derived from reading the letters to the Editor of *The Times*, recording the numerous and varied flowers picked by readers from their gardens in the depths of winter. E. A. Bowles, in *My Garden in Autumn and Winter* (1915), wrote: 'Last Christmas the garden went mad, Summer plants refused to go to bed, and Spring flowers woke up too early.' Violets and primroses, given mild weather, can be as much a part of winter as of spring.

Whatever the weather and the garden flowers consequently available or absent, there are certain commercially grown 'givens' for winter: 'Paperwhite' narcissi, for example, florists' chrysan-themums, forced anemones, tulips and irises. These are no less valuable because they are predictable, but responding to a larger range of winter's raw resources can bring new life to the display of these flowers, and provide completely unexpected floral delights.

*S*hown here are florists' hyacinths,
forced for winter flowering; red-barked
dogwood; Pekin, contorted, or curly willow;
pussy willow; large-leaved tree ivy and trailing stems
of yellow-variegated *Hedera helix* 'Goldheart' in a
state of readiness. Displayed *en masse*, the wispy
leafless branches balance the dense bulk of the
hyacinths, and dilute some of their 'fresh-from-the-
florist' perfection. For long-lasting displays, buy
hyacinths when the lowest florets are starting to
open; they appreciate several hours in a deep
container of water before being arranged.

*C*olour in the winter landscape is largely neutral, as reflected in this indoor display of dried cow parsley seed heads and pears. More colourful options include florists' flowers and flowers preserved with all or most of their colour intact. A nice compromise is to display florists' flowers, such as chrysanthemums or carnations, with stark winter branches or seed heads, as seasonal reference.

WINTER COLOURS

Most gardens are muted in winter, with the majority of plants dormant. Winter's palette is one of whites, blacks and neutrals: grey in shades of dove, silver, stone, slate, pearl, steel, pewter, opal, mist and charcoal; and soft browns and beiges in equally numerous shades. Whereas during the rest of the year the eye is bombarded with colour, winter is a season in which the eye works hard to search colour out. It is the season in which to find subtle interest in the most seemingly dull shades and tints. The colour of the winter sky in England is, more often than not, no colour at all, quite different from the clear blue winter skies of New England.

In northern temperate climates, winter means snow, and so by extension white is a particularly wintery colour. White has always been a symbol of purity, innocence and chastity; the white rose or white Madonna lily is symbolic of the Virgin Mary. As with other colours, white has contradictory connotations: of weddings, christenings and confirmations, events of pure joy, and of funerals. And though white-hot metal is hotter than red-hot metal, and the sun on a sunny day is an impossibly luminous white, white is visually cool, even cold, and aloof rather than friendly. White flowers are usually seen against green foliage, reinforcing the coolness. Coolness, whether visual or emotional, and sophistication are often linked: all-white interiors are often sophisticated, and because they are impractical and need much upkeep, often intimate wealth.

White is evocative of stillness and calm serenity, of nothingness and of potential: a blank sheet of paper waiting to be written on, a blank canvas to be painted, a lined wall to be papered. Technically, white is absence of colour and the presence of reflected light; snow, for example, appears white but is simply reflected light. Like snow, white daisy petals are composed of microscopic air pockets which reflect light in all directions, so they 'read' as white. When the air is removed from the petals and replaced with water, the petals appear transparent.

In displaying flowers, and also in interior design, white, like green, sometimes suffers second-class status. 'It's only white' is the lament of those wanting a blaze, or at least a flicker, of colour. And because white goes with everything, it is also sometimes frowned upon as an easy way out: in case of uncertainty, give or use white flowers. This, too, is an unfair burden for white to bear.

*A*rum, or calla, lilies, *Zantedeschia aethiopica* are South African, and in northern temperate climates are hardy in ponds in warm, sheltered gardens.
Their flowers are reminiscent of the 1890s' Aesthetic Movement, of which Oscar Wilde was the most famous proponent, and of Art Nouveau illustrations. Cut arums are heavy drinkers, and their water needs topping up regularly.

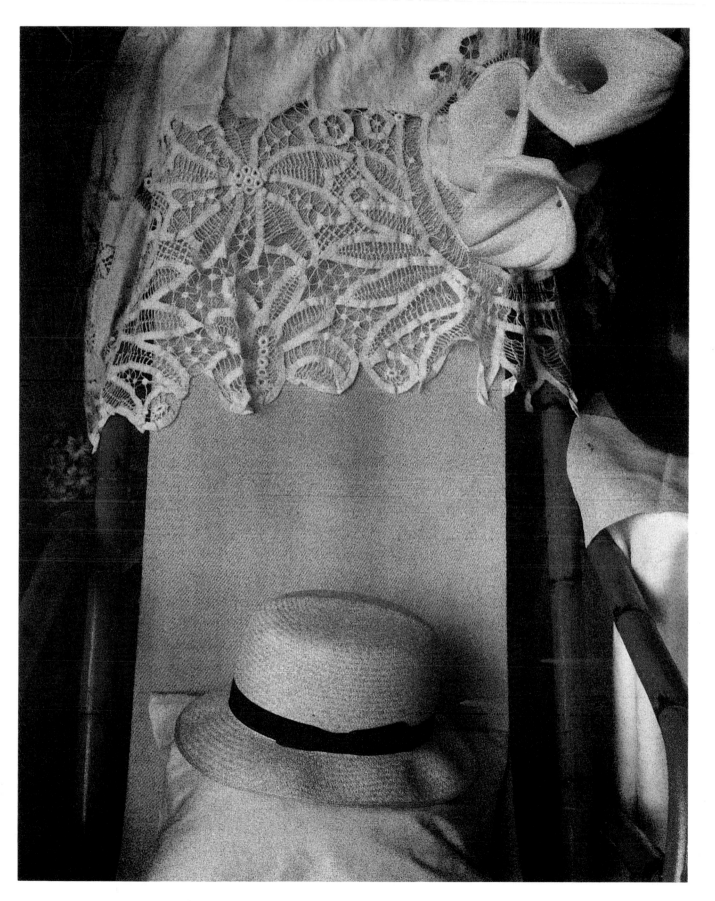

Although, technically, there is only one white, as opposed to, say, many pinks or yellows, observing white – white furniture, white walls, white paper, white china and white flowers – reveals that white varies. Some white flowers are flat and evenly dense in colour, for example Christmas roses and camellias. Other, often thinner-petalled, white flowers are translucent and tinged: white crocus, snowdrops and chincherinchee, for example. (The green tips and dots on snowdrop blossoms hint at their evolution from leaves.)

Form also affects how white is perceived. Intricate, multiple flower heads, such as white lilac, hydrangea and buddleia, contain tiny shadows between and within each floret, which break up the solidity of the white, introducing 'subtle variations. Huge, flat areas of white, such as the flower-like spathes of arums and spathiphyllums, can look artificial, even plastic.

There are many garden plants with white-variegated leaves, but some plants, such as horse chestnut and variegated holly, occasionally throw out branches of all-white leaves. Lacking chlorophyll, these genetically defective leaves could never support growth independent from the parent plant, but they are intriguing, nonetheless.

In the garden, the actuality of white can sometimes fall short of the ideal of white. White camellias, as an idea, are exquisite, but in fact are often brown edged or discoloured from harsh weather. White snow, as an idea, is exquisite, but in a city, even after a short time, is depressingly dingy and dirty. Because white is also symbolic of cleanliness, a marred or flawed white object is particularly disappointing.

Black, the opposite of white, represents the complete absorption of all visible light wavelengths. Black is evocative of old age, death, depression and sorrow: black moods, black despair. In fashion terms, black is sophisticated and formal: the little black dress, morning coats, tuxedos. Black is solemn, dramatic, especially in conjunction with white, severe and harsh. Black is also mysterious, the colour of the unknown: the dark side of the moon, the black holes said to exist in the universe.

Very little in the garden is actually black, but winter branches appear so, silhouetted against the pale sky. The idea of a black flower is intriguing but also slightly repugnant; many Americans who grew up in the Fifties and Sixties will remember the glamorous, nationally syndicated comic-strip heroine Brenda Starr, perpetually in search of her handsome boyfriend, who was, in turn, perpetually lost in the jungles of South America, in search of the fabled black orchid.

In real life there are no pure black flowers, though some are close, including the large, bearded blue-black iris 'Tuxedo'; the mourning iris, *I. susiana*, its deep-grey flowers blotched and veined with purple black; and the near-black spathes of *Arum palaestinum*. The near-black flowers of *Geranium phaeum*, the mourning widow; the maroon-black of certain violets, tulips and *Helleborus purpurascens* 'Ballard's Black'; and the dark central blotches on red tulip and poppy petals also 'read' as black.

A globe artichoke thistle adds a subtle shimmer of light to an indoor winter vignette. As with many long-cultivated plants, artichoke's generic name, *Cynara*, has mythological origins. A goddess, jealous of Cinara, a beautiful young maiden, turned her into an artichoke, and her island home became known as Cynara. *Kyon* is Greek for dog; a more mundane explanation is that the plant was so named because the protective bracts resembled dogs' teeth.

Grey is a particularly winter tone: cold, sunless light; noncommittal, anonymous, subtle and what you make of it. It is variously passive, humble, dignified, restrained and neutral, soothing or boring, according to personal mood and response. On the whole, grey does not go in and out of fashion, and in winter it is the general landscape backdrop against which all else is seen.

No flowers are grey, although some hellebores, especially Lenten rose (*Helleborus orientalis*) hybrids, have flowers of a greenish mauve approaching sombre grey. Grey foliage, such as that of artemisia and senecio, is usually associated with summer and warm Mediterranean climates. Tree bark is often grey, as are wild fungi, driftwood, pebbles, twigs, reindeer moss and weather-worn conifer cones – all raw materials for winter floral displays.

Primary and secondary hues and tints are also part of winter, if only a small part. In northern temperate climates, many winter

*N*arcissus, tulips, roses, polyanthus and cornflowers, having been preserved in silica gel, are presented as a memento of spring and summer. Preserving flowers in silica gel, sand or borax is an ancient practice, but more difficult than air drying to get right. Here, the blue of the polyanthus and cornflowers retains its pure hue; the pinks, reds and yellows are more muted.

*S*prays of the deep-pink moth orchid,
Phalaenopsis, and the more delicate
blooms of *Aranda* offer exotic winter colour
from the florist. Misting the flowers, changing the
water and re-cutting the stems regularly help extend
their life as cut flowers. Orchids that wilt
prematurely can often be revived by submerging
them in water for an hour.

flowers are bright yellow, seemingly radiating sunlight absorbed earlier in the year. These include winter jasmine, winter aconite, wintersweet, witch hazel, *Corylopsis* and *Mahonia*. There are pink viburnums, hellebores, daphnes, camellias, hardy cyclamen, bergenias and winter-flowering cherries, almonds and heathers; and the late winter blue of Algerian iris (*I. unguicularis*) and *I. reticulata*, followed by squills and the tiny blue bells of lungwort.

WINTER FRAGRANCE

Though less obvious than the heady fragrance of summer, winter fragrance, like colour, is there for those who search it out. Some bees are about in winter, and winter flowers still have to attract suitable pollinators; the huge, round seed pods of snowdrops attest to their success. Winter flowers are, on the whole, small, open in the daytime, and are most fragrant on warm, still, sunny days, when insects take to the wing.

Some of the most intensely fragrant winter-flowering shrubs are, unfortunately, coarse or dull-looking in growth habit and leaf, so are unsuitable for small or even medium-sized gardens. Among them is wintersweet, with its waxy yellow flowers. In Victorian and Edwardian times it was fashionable to collect the stemless flowers and float them, tightly packed, in shallow dishes of water, to scent a room. Other dull but fragrant winter shrubs include the winter-flowering honeysuckle, *Lonicera fragrantissima*, with its tiny white flowers; witch hazel, with spidery yellow, orange or scarlet flowers; and *Corylopsis* species, with hanging yellow, bell-like flowers. Even *Viburnum farreri*, a cottage-garden favourite, is not particularly beautiful as a plant.

There are exceptions. Species of evergreen winter box, or *Sarcococca*, are extremely shade tolerant and produces deliciously scented tiny white flowers against dainty, glossy green foliage; mahonias have an attractive growth habit, pinnate evergreen leaves and yellow flowers smelling of lily of the valley; and there are several evergreen and scented daphnes, *D. cneorum* being among the best.

Potpourri is especially welcome indoors in winter. It is a big seller at Christmas time, and left-overs are often half-price in the January sales. Jaded potpourri can be enhanced with a drop or two of a suitable essential oil, such as oil of rose, oil of lavender or oil of rose geranium. For more spicy blends, try combining powdered, crushed or whole spices, such as mace, cloves, cinnamon, coriander and fennel, with dried lemon or orange rinds. Indoors, the fragrance of ripe quince is also evocative of winter, and a big bowl of old-fashioned pear-shaped yellow quinces makes a long-lasting display. Quinces release enormous amounts of ethylene gas, however, which adversely affects cut flowers such as orchids, gypsophila and irises.

In a small room the fragrance of forced hyacinth, 'Paperwhite' narcissi and orange blossom can be so intense that it seems decadent. Fortunately (or unfortunately), flower fragrance fades indoors over the course of a day or two, or perhaps one just becomes more accustomed to it, and notices it less.

A garland of fresh ivy, swag of dried
Helichrysum, trumpet lilies and
pineapples make a pleasant, wintry
composition. The lily's sweet fragrance is lovely in
small doses but can be overpowering; though a daytime flower, it shares with night blooms, such as
datura and frangipani, a rich, decadent intensity.

Frosty in feeling if not in fact, a tidy row of figs are backed by an aromatic, dried flower wreath. The monochromatic scheme makes this an ideal subject for a pencil sketch, as a study in textural contrasts. Incorporated in the wreath are wormwood, sage, rosemary, santolina and thyme, which emit a fresh, astringent aroma when handled.

WINTER BERRIES

*P*otpourris are especially welcome in winter, for colour as much as fragrance. A few drops of essential oils can refresh potpourris with jaded scent; the addition of a few freshly dried petals can enliven those with faded colour or those, such as lavender, with naturally bland tones.

The reds of many berries enliven the winter scene: holly, pyracantha, cotoneaster, *Aucuba japonica*, skimmia and *Sorbus* 'Winter Cheer'. And as with white flowers, the white of 'white' berries also varies. Mistletoe berries are translucent, overlaid with palest green and slightly sinister in appearance. (Kissing under the mistletoe is said to have an aphrodisiac effect, a left-over from the earlier belief that mistletoe induced fertility, due to the similarity of the clustered berries to male genitals.) The opaque, marble-like berries of symphoricarpos, or snowberry, have no such connotations; though dull shrubs in the growing season, their berries persist well into winter, adding spark to displays of cut evergreen foliage or flowers. The white berries of *Pernettya mucronata* are so densely packed on the stems that they suffer from the 'too much of a good thing' syndrome. Weighed down by its own berries, the plant loses all natural grace, and in providing an ever bigger splash of colour, becomes a sort of one-plant freak show. (The same is unfortunately true of the pink-, crimson- purple- and black-berried varieties of pernettya.)

There are many garden and wild berries approximating black in various degrees. Privet produces glossy black berries; stripped of its leaves and used in cut-flower displays, it becomes far more exotic looking than in its normal role as garden hedging. (Stripping the leaves from spotted laurel or holly branches puts their clusters of red berries in another, more exotic-looking light.) Mahonia berries are

A wine glass contains the berries and evergreen foliage of the cottage-garden favourite, laurustinus (*Viburnum tinus*). In northern temperate climates, laurustinus flowers more prolifically than it fruits, but privet, mahonia, barberry and wild elderberry, bullace, sloe and blackberry provide more generous alternative material in a similar, rich shade.

blue-tinged black, as are many barberries. Ripe ivy berries are black, and the tidy, rounded clusters look machine-made in their perfection. Many viburnums have blue-black berries: *V. davidii*, *V. tinus*, *V. rhytidophyllum* and *V. prunifolium*, the so-called black haw, whose fruits are used in preserves.

The production of berries depends on many factors: weather, especially that of the previous summer; the presence of male plants and suitable pollinators in the case of species such as skimmia and holly, in which male and female flowers are borne on separate plants; and whether heavy crops were produced the previous year, in which case there will probably be fewer the following year. Once winter berries are produced, birds are the main adversaries. (Few people would go to the trouble of netting or caging ornamental berries in the way that strawberries and raspberries are protected, but cutting sprigs of berried holly in October and storing them in the cold could, however, be considered fair game.) As far as birds' preferences go, red berries are often, but not always, eaten first. Other factors include the order of ripening and palatability. The red hips of the dog rose (*Rosa canina*), for example, tend to be left until the tastier hips of the field rose (*Rosa arvensis*) have been eaten, while the unpleasant red berries of the guelder rose (*Viburnum opulus*) are avoided. Blackberries and ripe elderberries are always popular, but the presumably less tasty and later-ripening black berries of ivy are eaten as a last resort, in March and April.

WINTER FOLIAGE

Of all the seasons, winter is when one is most dependent on foliage for indoor displays, and garden foliage, with all its imperfections, is particularly valuable for offsetting the anonymous perfection of florists' flowers. Those without gardens can closely watch the activities of gardeners in public parks; evergreen prunings that would otherwise be discarded, if freshly gathered and conditioned, can add character to a mixed display, or form a display on their own.

Conifers are winter stalwarts, but many are sombre, and cypress and yew are funereal in connotation. The solitary sprigs of cypress or false cypress automatically included in mixed winter bunches from florists' shops are the foliage equivalent of the solitary sprigs of gypsophila: symbolic rather than useful, perhaps the vestigial remains from more generous times.

Beautiful conifers, such as cryptomeria and juniper, are slow-growing and not sold commercially as cut foliage. Pine branches are good for large-scale displays, but their curving shapes have wills of their own and are difficult to use in smaller arrangements. Then, too, most pine trees shed their lower branches as they grow, making it difficult to reach any for cutting. Dwarf pines and other dwarf conifers are easy to reach, but so slow-growing that cutting foliage for indoor display is sacrilege. Blue spruce, sold at Christmas, is among the nicest cut winter foliage, used intact or broken into small sprays, for combining with florists' daffodils, tulips and irises.

Broad-leaved evergreens provide more potential: generally, the smaller the leaf, the wider is the range of its uses in cut displays. *Choisya ternata*, or Mexican orange, is a suitable candidate for the 'one-shrub' garden. Its aromatic, three-part leaves are glossy and when crushed release a slightly bitter smell reminiscent of rue and citrus fruit, to which it is related; it is shade tolerant and carries pretty white flowers, on and off, all year. Bay, evergreen oak, eleagnus, box, arbutus, pittosporum, camellia, pieris, cotoneaster, pyracantha and evergreen viburnums provide good winter foliage, though only box and pittosporum are normally carried by florists.

Portuguese laurel foliage, a glossy, evergreen small-scale version of cherry leaves, is useful for cut displays but not widely grown. Holly has an annoying habit of producing sparse tufts of leaves along its curving stems; these can be cut up for small-scale displays, or camouflaged by other, more heavily clothed branches.

Hebe foliage is unique: with its leaves neatly arranged up the branches it has the appearance of having been designed by art students rather than having evolved naturally. Rue may be listed either as a shrub or a perennial in gardening books and catalogues. Its lacy, nearly evergreen foliage looks particularly blue in cold weather, and though never a large source of foliage, a tiny sprig or two can enliven a bunch of violets or snowdrops, or a twig of *Viburnum farreri*.

Garrya elliptica, with its pendant grey male catkins, is the *sine qua non* of many flower arrangers' gardens. Bad weather can disfigure the evergreen leaves, but in good condition the plant is

No flowers are needed in this study of winter neutrals enlivened by a generous bunch of *Malus*, pomegranates and Russet apples (unpromising in appearance but exquisitely refreshing). Sweet chestnuts and a hen pheasant awaiting gutting and hanging prop the vignette, set against the antique floral-patterned curtain and wooden screen.

indispensable, whether huge branches or tiny twigs are used.

Large-leaved evergreens such as laurel, *Magnolia grandiflora* and rhododendron, can be awkward to incorporate into ordinary-sized mixed displays. Laurel and evergreen magnolia leaves tend to grow in flat planes, so they don't 'sit' comfortably with other material; rhododendron leaves often grow in limp clusters separated by barren lengths of stem. In a large container, however, the foliage displayed on its own can be impressive.

Given reasonable weather, cut foliage can also come from deciduous woody plants. Summer-flowering jasmine, for example, often holds its leaves until Christmas, and twining jasmine round and through florists' flowers can counteract their anonymity. Other good subjects for twining include lesser and greater periwinkle, spotted dead-nettle (*Galeobdolon luteum*) and even, *in extremis*, the dreaded weed ground ivy (*Glechoma hederacea*). Its slender runners and glossy, small, round leaves are charming, and belie its ruthless invasiveness. (Ground ivy was, before hops, the chief bitter flavouring of ale; it was taken to New England and grown for this purpose, and for its medicinal value as a cleanser.)

Large round bergenia leaves are delightful with garden or florists' flowers, and many epimedium species have leaves that turn

Christmassy without being coy or saccharine, a generously full red, green and white display of florists' anemones, heavily fragrant white Amazon lilies, *Eucharis grandiflora*, defoliated holly berries, ivy and bindweed foliage (above), and on a smaller scale without foliage (left). A cluster of red glasses, dried umbellifer seed heads, candlesticks and a sculpted angel provide the props for this seasonal and mildly symbolic vignette.

russet in winter, an ideal contrast for pale pink flowers. In midwinter, shiny, arrow-shaped leaves are produced by lords and ladies, *Arum maculatum*, and *A. italicum*. The cultivars *A. i.* 'Pictum' and 'Marmoratum' are particularly beautiful, their dark-green leaves marbled with white. The name 'lords and ladies' comes from the obvious sexual symbolism of the flower, an upright spadix enfolded in a spathe. (Nature occasionally displays a sense of humour, perhaps irony: the pollinators of lords and ladies are female dung midges, drawn by the foul smell of dung produced by the flowers.) The towers of densely packed scarlet berries that follow in autumn are long-lasting and cheering, and as useful for indoor displays as the leaves. Another unusually early herbaceous perennial with attractive foliage for cutting is *Valeriana phu* 'Aurea' whose young leaves are bright yellow, turning green as they age.

Florists' ferns are often used, like sprigs of cypress, as token greenery. Ferns in bulk have more to offer, but must usually be home-grown or collected. There are many evergreen and some deciduous ferns which last well into winter before turning brown. The hart's-tongue fern, holly fern and polypody fern are lovely at this time of year; the prickly shield fern and male fern also retain their fresh green colour until the new fronds appear in spring.

WINTER BRANCHES

A selection of evergreen and ever-grey garden foliage, especially valuable in winter. From the left, variegated *Euonymus fortunei radicans*, *Senecio* 'Sunshine', *Hebe pinguifolia* 'Pagei', *Rosmarinus officinalis* and *Camellia japonica*, on a bed of blue spruce, *Picea pungens glauca*. A 'token' flower, *Lilium longiflorum*, is included, but massed mixed foliage can be beautiful displayed on its own.

Cut branches against a white or solid-coloured wall indoors are reminiscent of trees against the sky. The unnaturally twisted branches of *Corylus avellana* 'Contorta' and *Salix matsudana* 'Tortuosa', are so popular that they are almost clichés, joining the ranks of radicchio and Porsche as symbols of success on a certain level. Quite ordinary shrubs and trees produce interesting leafless branches, too, without the burden of symbolic overtones: kerria, oak, birch, hornbeam and beech, for example. The black buds of ash and the huge sticky buds of horse chestnut are each unique, and destroy the fallacy that all leafless branches look alike.

Branches with brightly coloured bark, such as red- and yellow-barked dogwood, red-barked alder, and red-, golden- and purple-barked willow sometimes look more colourful in the winter garden, when lit by the sun and seen against a subdued backdrop, than when cut and brought indoors. Nevertheless, they are still worthwhile additions to cut-flower displays, and also pleasing on their own. On a small scale, the slender, wiry, bare green branches of wild bilberry add character to displays of florists' or garden flowers.

The Japanese art of Ikebana, which dates from the sixth century, is particularly suited to winter, since little material is used,

Lichen-covered larch branches, forced hazel in catkin, and white-painted umbellifer seed pods provide a large, linear display. Hazel catkins carry the male flowers, and each catkin releases literally millions of pollen grains in the wind. (It is no wonder that hazel was a symbol of fertility in medieval times!) The bud-like, petal-less female flowers are far less showy, with their tiny, crimson-red stigmas.

and branches play at least as important a role as flowers. Ikebana is hugely complex, with various schools and styles, and enormous mystic symbolism is attached to the choice, combination and positioning of material. Some of the basic tenets, though, can be extracted and applied to western displays. Observing the number of variations possible in arranging a few branches in a container, for example, or even the placement of one branch, is an exercise in refinement; working with minimal material instead of avoiding problems by adding more and more is a big challenge.

Ikebana also allows for judicious pruning, to remove twigs that are confusing or extraneous to the line of the branch, so possibilities are further enlarged. And the Oriental stress on seasonal and readily available material, as opposed to the forced or rare, is convenient and economical, as well as philosophically pure.

In Ikebana, branches never lean against the rim of a container, but are supported by a metal base, wooden fixer or forked twig in the neck of a container, to simulate natural growth. Florists' foam and wire-mesh netting are easy alternatives, but many Oriental shops stock the proper fixers and bases. Symmetry is avoided, and a more subtle asymmetrical balance and clarity of line is aimed for. Three components often feature, whether three branches or a mixture of branch, flower and foliage said to represent, heaven, earth and man. The principal component is tallest; the secondary component is half way in height between the principal and tertiary, or shortest component. To the western eye, as well as the Oriental, three is an inherently attractive number visually, and one with a powerful religious symbolism of its own.

WINTER CONTAINERS AND COVERINGS

In many homes, flowering houseplants replace cut flowers as a source of winter floral colour: cineraria, polyanthus, chrysanthemum, cyclamen, azalea, poinsettia, hippeastrum and forced hyacinth, narcissus and crocus. Plastic flowerpots, being cheap, lightweight, easily stacked, disinfected and replaced, have commercial advantages but no visual ones, and smack of disposability. Transferring a houseplant from a plastic to a terracotta pot makes it look more permanent and gives it more stability. A collection of ceramic cachepots and woven baskets provides more options, and grouping several pot plants of the same species in one container makes a greater impact than scattering them about.

Fresh sphagnum moss, covering the surface of the potting compost of houseplants and filling the space between the inner and outer container, helps conserve moisture and creates the pleasant illusion that the plant has recently come in from outdoors. With several plants in a single outer container, a packing and covering of moss makes a little landscape. Fresh sphagnum moss is available from florists; bun moss, a lovely alternative, grows on banks under trees and on roofs. In winter, bun moss is often dislodged from roofs by birds looking for insects, and handfuls of it may be collected from the ground immediately below them.

An old wooden trug, filled with lichen-covered larch branches and slender, cone-studded larch twigs. Larch is one of the few deciduous conifers; its spring growth is soft, milky-green, becoming old-gold in autumn. Like hazel, female larch flowers are wind pollinated, and have no decorative value in cut displays. Once pollinated, however, they develop into attractive brown, scaly cones, with the delicacy of diminutive, hand-carved wooden roses.

*S*hown here are Victorian earthenware jugs featuring Bacchanalian scenes, filled with fresh Turk's-cap ranunculus; a garden trug filled with dried roses, larkspur and hydrangeas; and a reflective plate of dried paeonies, perfectly preserved by the silica-gel method. Combining fresh and dried material in a single winter display increases one's options. By retaining the dried material but varying the fresh flowers and containers, and painting or chalking the gourds, the mood can be altered.

WINTER INSPIRATIONS, OBSERVATIONS AND PROJECTS

Long, dark nights and inclement weather make winter an inward-looking season, a frightening prospect for some, an exciting or serene one for others. It is a challenging time for creating cut-flower displays, but not without hope: even such unpromising winter venues as supermarkets can be a source of material. Gardenless urbanites can buy fat bunches of moss-curled parsley; heads of curly, or Batavian, endive; sprigs of rosemary and bunches of watercress, all useful in cut-flower displays if kept cool and with a few drops of bleach added to the water. Use parsley with florists' anemones, whose own foliage is parsley-like. Use rosemary as a foil for winter pinks, whose own foliage is soft grey-green and spiky. Batavian endive can counteract the predictability of florists' chrysanthemums.

Even if it is just by looking out of a window, observe the many different whites on a snowy day. Observe the different whites of flowers, such as forced tulips, chincherinchees, roses, lilies and 'Paperwhite' narcissi. Hold each one up to a white sheet of paper, observing the contrasts and shadows.

Observe the silhouettes of bare trees against the sky, both the outlines of branches and the density and quality of the internal framework. Observe how woody plants in close proximity affect each other's habit of growth.

Collect branches from two or three different trees or shrubs. Draw each branch in pencil or pen, then draw the spaces between the branches. Try a contour drawing of one branch. Look neither at the paper nor lift your pen or pencil from the time you begin drawing until you finish, making a single, continuous line which captures the flow, if not the exact proportions, of the branch. Finally, draw an imaginary branch, with a smooth, consistent flow from main to secondary branches, and from secondary branches to twigs.

Halve or quarter a winter cauliflower or tight head of cabbage, and draw it in detail. Compare the structure to that of tree branches.

In late winter, cut branches and bring them indoors to watch the leaf buds open. Quite ordinary species will do: sycamore, for example, or thorn. With cut branches of alder, hazel, *Garrya elliptica* and willow in bud, you can observe the lengthening catkins. Arrange an outer circle of florists' flowers around a central mass of bare twigs, then reverse the pattern and arrange a low frill of twigs around a central mass of cut flowers.

Collect various barks, dead tree roots and dead stems of tree ivy. Stripped of bark and bleached, whether naturally or artificially, tree-ivy stems make sculptural components in cut-flower displays. Fill a shallow bowl with rounded, water-washed pebbles or flints and granite chippings, add water and display upright sprigs of winter-flowering shrubs, or flowers cut from winter-flowering bulbs or perennials, inserted between the stones.

Make an indoor bulb garden. Buy small pots of winter-flowering irises, snowdrops, winter aconites, crocuses, miniature narcissi and species cyclamen in bud from a garden centre. Plant them in a large, shallow container, covering the surface of the potting compost

oinsettias, mistletoe and conifer cones
are traditional Christmas decorations,
and lend themselves to massed display. The
bright red, pink or white poinsettia 'petals' are
actually colourful leaf-like bracts; the flowers are
visually insignificant. For more adventurous
displays, gently remove the plant from its pot, wash
out the potting compost under running water, then
use as 'cut' flowers, with holly or red-barked
dogwood or willow.

with moss. (The Edwardians used to create tiny indoor winter gardens by sprinkling wheat or other grasses, such as canary grass, *Phalaris canariensis*, on a shallow bed of damp moss, and watch it germinate and grow.) Acorns and horse chestnuts can be half-buried in moss and germinated, for a miniature indoor forest.

Pot up clumps of snowdrops in bud from the garden, and bring them indoors to flower. When they finish flowering, divide the clumps and replant them in the garden.

Insert sprigs of holly, eleagnus and conifer into an evenly shaped potato until it is completely hidden, and hang it up as a room decoration. (Before the advent of florists' foam blocks, potatoes were often used as foundations for Christmas foliage decorations.)

Use houseplants to provide foliage for cut flowers. Sprigs of wax, or fairy, begonia and tradescantia root in water, and can add leafiness to, for example, a bunch of violets or snowdrops. The large velvety leaves of African violet can be used in the same way, and they also root in water.

Cluster leafy houseplants, in their pots, around a central glass filled with daffodils, winter anemones or Turks'-cap ranunculus.

Use cut foliage as 'props' for flowering houseplants. The huge trumpet flowers of hippeastrum, for example, are so mesmerizing that one forgets about the ludicrous length and often peculiar angles of their bare stems. Surround the stems with masses of broad-leaved evergreen foliage, or leafless branches with attractively coloured bark, so that the flowers seem to emerge from a forest of growth. Surround a small or oddly shaped azalea, as they often are, with a thick ruff or collar of cut greenery in several small glass tumblers.

WINTER TIPS

To force spring-flowering trees and shrubs in winter, wait until buds are showing, ideally after a stretch of cold weather. Those picked in midwinter can take a month or more to open; the closer to normal flowering time when the branches are cut, the quicker the flowers open. Scrape 2.5cm (1in) of bark away from the bottom of the cut stems, or hammer them, then dip them in 2.5cm (1in) of boiling water for a few seconds, and follow with a long drink of warm water. Many members of the *Rosaceae* family can be forced: crab apple, plum, cherry, peach, almond and pear, both ornamental and fruiting. Magnolia, Japanese quince, forsythia, winter jasmine and flowering currant can also be forced; forced flowers tend to be paler and less heavily scented than those that open naturally.

Submerge bergenia, dead-nettle and fern foliage in water for several hours before using. Submerge arum foliage, first adding a little starch to the water. Dip the cut ends of epimedium foliage in boiling water for a few seconds, before giving it a long drink.

Re-cut and hammer the ends of woody evergreen and berrying branches, then give them a long drink.

To keep camellia blossom fresh, place it in water as soon as possible after picking, and mist-spray regularly. This also helps with hellebores.

*T*hese dried mop-head hydrangeas are lit by candles in an antique candelabrum, softly reflected in an old mirror. Dried flowers, foliage and seed pods are as much a part of winter floral decoration as they are of autumnal displays. Dried hydrangeas in soft, muted blues, greys and greens are particularly cool and wintry in appearance, compared with the summery clear blues of dried larkspur.

• Submerge violets for a few hours before arranging, and overnight if they are to be displayed in a warm room.

• The most brightly coloured bark is normally produced on young wood; annual or biennial spring pruning of coloured-bark dogwoods, willows and brambles is a good idea.

• When buying a garden shrub for its berries, find out whether the species produces male and female flowers on separate plants. If so, buy at least one male to pollinate the female plants, which produce the berries.

A thought-provoking study of life and death in the floral world. The hippeastrum just coming into growth is displayed with silica-gel-preserved hippeastrum flowers. In late Victorian times, hybridizing hippeastrums became fashionable, just when hybridizing polyanthus, pansies and tulips went out of fashion, as being artificial and unnatural! Hippeastrums remain popular because they are reliable (the first year, in any case) and fun to observe developing. Flowering in second and later years depends on careful managing, including an induced period of dormancy after the foliage dies back.

INDEX

ACKNOWLEDGEMENTS

It has been a great pleasure taking the pictures for this book and I'm sorry it's over. I thank many people everywhere whose love and dedication to flowers has helped them once again to flourish and regain a firm place in our lives. My special thanks for Deborah Patterson, my friend and assistant. To the many people who gave so generously their help and encouragement, I say thank you.

The author and publishers would like to thank the Antique Collectors' Club Ltd for their kind permission to quote from *Home and Garden* and *Wood and Garden* by Gertrude Jekyll, and Oxford University Press to quote from *Lark Rise to Candleford* by Flora Thompson (OUP, 1954).

All photographs by Linda Burgess

Special thanks to Kirsten and Bob Jones, Ingrid and Bill Mason, and Maggie and Mike Paterson for allowing us to photograph in their homes; to Wheatcroft Roses for providing the roses on pages 58–9, available from Wheatcroft Garden Centre, Edwalton, Nottingham; and to Dennis France of Ropsely, Lincs, for his assistance.

The publishers and photographer would also like to thank the following for kindly supplying props for special photography:

The Gallery of Antique
    Costume and Textiles
2 Church Street
London NW8
Tel: 01-723-9981

Tobias and the Angel
68 White Hart Lane
London SW13
Tel: 01-878-8902

Stitches and Daughters
5–7 Tranquil Vale
Blackheath Village
London SE3
Tel: 01-852-8507

Putnams
1 Matthew Yard
29 Shorts Gardens
London WC2
Tel: 01-431-2935

Robert Young Antiques
68 Battersea Bridge Road
London SW11
Tel: 01-228-7847

Mrs Munro
11 Montpelier Street
London SW7
Tel: 01-589-5052

Mary Rose Young
Oak House
Arthurs Folly
Parkend
Lydney
Glos. Gl15 4JQ
Tel: 0594-563425

Still Life
58 Tranquil Vale
London SE3
Tel: 01-463 9353

Jouventin
Chenil Galleries
183 Kings Road
London SW3
Tel: 01-351-5353

Judy Greenwood Antiques
657 Fulham Road
London SW6
Tel: 01-736 6037